Tales from the Dundee Tenements

# Dae Yeh Mind Thon Time?

## MAE STEWART

BLACK & WHITE PUBLISHING

First published 2009
by Black & White Publishing Ltd
29 Ocean Drive, Edinburgh EH6 6JL

1 3 5 7 9 10 8 6 4 2    09 10 11 12 13

ISBN: 978 1 84502 272 3

Typeset by RefineCatch Limited, Bungay, Suffolk
Printed and bound by CPI Cox & Wyman, Reading

# Dae Yeh Mind Thon Time?

# CONTENTS

# CONTENTS

# INTRODUCTION

These reminiscences are a compilation of my own personal childhood and teenage memories of life in an industrial city, my hometown of Dundee, from the mid 1940s to the late 1950s.

For those of you who are old enough to say 'I remember that' then I hope this is an excursion down memory lane for you too.

For those of you who are too young to remember a world without television, then wouldn't you like to explore, just for a while, a world that didn't have inside toilets, or even electric lights, and glance at what life was like back then?

Apart from the material side of things, I bet you'll recognise yourself in half the predicaments I landed in when I was a kid.

For those of you who think that as you don't live north of the Border, or live in another part of Scotland, that you wouldn't understand half the jargon . . . well, as inhabitants of the same planet, we all share the same hopes and aspirations, coping strategies, ups and downs, and the desire to be happy. Managing when you have to because 'Whit else kin yeh dae?' And laughing whenever you get the chance.

Anyway, I believe you can learn the basics of another language, such as Spanish, in seventy-two hours.

That said, I'm sure we can join hands dialectally 'fir the next wee while as weh roam aroond they pages'.

Mae Stewart

# DEDICATION

For my parents Mary and John Stewart

# THE START O' ME

I was born in an attic, up an outside wooden stair, early on an April morning in 1940. The street was up the West End of the city. You'll find a Dundee University Campus there now.

I moved homes when I was just months old, to a two-roomed ground floor tenement flat along the road, in a wee cul-de-sac called the 'Warkie Roadie' (Work Road), so named because it used to be the main entrance to one of the jute mills in that area.

My first play area was cindered ground and a pavement. But I did spend a lot of time going with my Mother to 'The Meddlie' (Magdalene Green), a huge green area just about ten minutes away from where we lived.

My tenement was on one side of the cul-de-sac, and an eight-feet-high mill wall was on the other side. The wall surrounded the mill building, which had a huge chimney stack that cast its shadow over the whole cul-de-sac.

The mill was still alive then; we could always hear its heart-beat. The huge mill stack that towered over everything else must've blown forth smoke every day, but I can't seem to remember noticing the smoke that much.

There was also a dead pond attached to the mill, surrounded by barbed wire, and we were forbidden to go near it because it was too dangerous so, of course, it became a magnet for every kid in the street and, if you could escape the million and one eyes that lived in our street, then you had to go see for yourself.

I remember being frog-marched home with my older brother one day because my father had come up the road from his work and spotted us ballet dancing around the wall that surrounded the 'auld pondie'.

I think I started crying and declaring 'Eh promise Eh'll no dae it aghen' before even a word was said to me in the hope that there would be no comeback for this disobedience.

But there was!

The top of the cul-de-sac was framed by a huge mill door that had been blocked up when they'd built a new mill entrance just round the corner. The huge door had three concrete steps up to it. That door was there for me to use as castles, mansions, hotels, and theatre stages; anything I wanted, and where we all played to our hearts' content.

I lived next door to my maternal grandmother, and aunts and uncles all lived nearby.

My grannies' house conjoined one of the mill walls. I remember as a child hearing the distant *rickety-rick . . . rickety-rick . . . rickety-rick . . . rickety-rick* of the looms from one of the working sheds next door. And if you stood out in the cul-de-sac then you could hear the looms and the machinery quite clearly from over the factory wall.

As a young girl, I chose to work in the mills for a short spell, and I can tell you the noise is deafening. But I had a choice, whereas my grandmother's generation had none.

My tenement was four storeys high, plus the attics. Each landing had one pokey outside toilet. Ours was up at the end of our closie, for use by all the ground-floor residents. If memory serves me, about thirteen to fifteen people shared my toilet.

Mind you, the outside toilet never bothered me, apart from in the winter when it was 'in-business-oot', before you froze to bits. But, it *was* one of the few places you could be on your own. That is, until someone first enquired (more than once in my case), 'Anybody in?'

The fact that the door was closed and bolted never stopped folk from saying this. Then they'd eventually hammer the door: 'Hurry up. Eh'm burstin.' Then you'd to be as quick as you could, but until then you could just sit and while away the time singing to yourself, or listening to what was going on outside the door. In fact, our door had a wee hole that you could spy through and see what was going on in the closie as well.

Toilet paper was indeed small pieces of newspaper cut up into squares and hung on a wire hook on the wall. That was the norm back then.

But my mother always insisted we had toilet paper. The type that was in that wee green box called Izal I think, and we kept it in the house. I never liked the Izal much I have to say, and never bothered with it.

Our 'ben-the-room windie' looked out on to the drying green and the toilet sat at the side of the green. In the cold weather my mother used to slide us over the window sill and we'd run across to the toilet. That saved us having to run outside and up the closie.

My Auntie Mary, who lived in Hill Street, had her own inside toilet, so you could spend even more time in there, until she shouted, 'Is thir anybody died in there?'

I remember asking my father, 'How kin we no live in a hoose weh an inside lavvie?'

His reply. 'Nae problem! Jist you hing on, an Eh'll stick a bucket in the wardrobe!'

Our house had two rooms which were about fourteen feet

by twelve feet (if they were that). The kitchen had a bed recess, in which my parents slept. When my youngest sister was born, she slept at the bottom of the bed, in a wicker clothes basket, lined with a white towel. Some infants I knew slept in the bottom drawer of the kitchen dresser. The drawer was left open, of course!

My elder sister, my two brothers and I slept in the only other room.

I slept on a Rexene fold-down settee with my eldest sister. My wee brother slept in a Rexene fold-down chair bed. My big brother slept on the floor on a 'shakie-doon', a mattress that was rolled out at night and was stuck behind the wardrobe during the day.

One of my earliest memories is hearing the seven o'clock mill siren ('bummer' to us) calling everybody to work. I do not know where the word 'bummer' comes from. It must have been a real bummer right enough, having to get up so early, rain, hail or snow, and go to work. Back then, it really was a case of work or want, so folk had to turn out in all weather no matter what.

In my grandparents' day they worked a twelve-hour, five-and-a-half day week, working six hours on Saturday. The money they were paid was a pittance. Many mill workers were injured by unprotected machinery as there was no health and safety. To say it was a hard life does not do it honour.

Large numbers of men in my community also worked at the docks, or in the shipyard. My own Father was a 'sparkie' with the Caledon Yard for many years. 'The Boatyaird' was a way of life and is a whole other story in itself.

Everything in my world was right on the doorstep: bakers; butchers; wee general stores (called 'Johnnie-a-things'); fruit shops; chip shops; ice cream shops; schools; churches and church halls; the Labour Party Rooms (I don't think there

4

were any Conservative Party Halls in my neck of the woods).

And . . . we knew everybody, and everybody knew us.

So there you have it! That was my first world, the place where I started out on my journey and where I spent the first nine years of my life. It was my training ground.

As an adult I came to realise just how valuable a training ground it was, and how fortunate I was to have been born into my family. It equipped me for the ups and downs that life would have in store for me, and gave me a faith in myself, and others, that cannot be bought.

As a child, I did not have the luxuries that are provided today, but I did not feel in the least bit deprived. Sure there were things I couldn't get because the money was just not there, but I had the strength of my parents, friends and family, and the folk who surrounded me. I am privileged to have had such an honorable and steadfast background to start me out in life.

My parents (and many others just like them), who had little financially or just enough, shared with each other bigger dreams. They aspired to much more for their children and worked very hard, to make these hopes become a reality.

\* \* \*

Many years later, I remember having a conversation with my mother, who had survived some of the hardships of her own early childhood (which was not uncommon in her days) as one of the most humorous and upbeat persons I ever knew, without one ounce of self-pity:

Yeh ken Ma, when Eh look roond aboot me now, an see whit weh've a got – cars; telephones; wardrobes a jam packed – it maks me realise how little material things

5

weh hid when Eh wiz a bairn. An yet Eh never felt Eh wiz the least bit depreheved or anything like that.

She gave me one of her 'Eh canna believe Eh heard that' looks and replied:

If yeh hiv tae ask the question, wiz Eh depreheved? Then yeh most definitely wer'na. Thir wiz some times, when Eh wiz wee, meh meal wiz a tattie an some margarine, or a plate o chips. An when yeh hid tae wear second-hand clahes, or some ither bugger's hand-me-doons, then yeh dinna hae tae ask if yeh wir sometimes depreheved.

So there you have it. The start o' me. A very ordinary, normal working class, start to life, just like hundreds of us in my times.

What makes it appear extraordinary to me as an adult, and looking back on it all from the life I have now, is how my mother and father paved the road for me, and how they sacrificed, protected and cushioned me along the way. And shoved me when they felt they had to.

For that they will always have my eternal respect, love, and gratitude.

# SUNDAYS DOON
# BEH THE WAHTER

I have always loved living beside the River Tay, and am fortunate to have had a view of this beautiful span of water every day of my life. When I lived up the West End a hive of activities went on all along the Esplanade at the river side.

It was just ten minutes from our house to the Meddlie and the Esplanade. Its Sunday name was Magdalene Green.

I have memories of going there in the summer with my mother and my brother who was still in the Tansad (or pushchair, if you're not as ancient as I am) so I must have been pre-school. She would take a picnic and I would run wild, and get her all to myself.

On Sundays, in the good weather, folk would all have a walk down to the Meddlie and have a blether. There would be football 'ower the bridge', which would be over the railway lines and on to the Esplanade, and the men would gather and either form their own teams, watch the youngsters or the juniors, or 'jist hiv a kick aboot'.

Then, of course, there was a bandstand right in the centre of the Meddlie, and sometimes there would be entertainment there. A band would play or, on occasions, there would be Highland dancers. There was an old blind woman who used to sing and play a wee organ there some Sundays as well.

But I loved the bandstand best when it was empty. For then I could be anything I liked in that bandstand. And it made a perfect stage, posh house, ship, or anything else you could imagine.

Folk used to swim in the Tay on Sundays in the good weather. I believe some folk used to even dive off the wall, even in the winter. And although it's horses for courses, I have never understood why you'd want to jump into icy water at any time at all.

However, my father, who was an excellent swimmer, was part of a swimming club that was created by a group of folks who met along the Esplanade at the weekends. They built their changing huts on the pavement adjacent to the sea wall.

I can remember, as a kid, watching him and others swim out to the sand banks and then swim back. They had a race called the Tay Swim, and they would swim to Fife from the Dundee side. I think he must have won it once for I remember this fancy green glass dressing table set he'd been presented with adorning our dressing table and him getting pride of place.

He used to tell us about going down for a swim really early on Sundays. He would take a wax cloth bag he'd made, that had a string on it for going round his waist. He would swim out with his pals to one of the sand banks and just lie there quietly and wait for the seals to come up and have a nosey, and then throw food to them.

He said that it took quite a while for the seals to come over to them, but after that they must have realised that my father and his pals were in their territory and came on to the sand banks no bother at all. They even ate out of their human counterparts' hands once they were all fish together.

8

There was a Victorian swimming pool along nearer the City Centre end of the Tay, and many a happy hour I spent there. Once more at the weekends you had to queue to get in.

There was no such word as unisex anything back then, in fact I would've got it in the neck for saying the word 'sex' out loud when I was a kid. We thought 'sex' were bags they delivered the tatties in.

So it was the Ladies Pool and the Gents Pool, but the kids got to melee in together and I loved it. I can't remember the time before my father taught me to swim.

There was a ferry service operated not far along from the swimming baths, and a proud boast I used to have about that was, 'Eh've got an uncle that drehves ane o' the Fifies'.

These boats sailed from Dundee to Fife on a regular basis in the summertime. One of my uncles was a sailor during the war, and when he came home he got a job on one of the four boats that used to make these journeys over the water.

In the good weather there was as big a queue to get on the Fifie, as there was to get on the bus to Broughty Ferry. You were issued with a wee blue ticket at the ticket office and then walked along the cobbled quay and on to the boat.

I used to love going upstairs on the boat and feeling the wind in my hair. It was just like being a pirate. Then, if my uncle was taking that boat over, I would get in to the cabin to watch them steering it into berth at the other side.

So we'd get off at the Quay at Wormit and spend the day walking along the beach in Fife, or having a picnic on a grassy bit.

Folk used to go along by the Esplanade to the pebbled beach near Kingoodie Quarry and gather 'wulks' (whelks if you lived in far-off London). I have vague recollections of going there with my grandfather (he died when I was quite wee) and discovering that when you boiled the wulks in a pot they were sometimes still alive. I about had a fit and I haven't eaten one from that day to this.

It was on my travels along to the Ninewells that I first encountered the tents that made up the wee encampment that housed the tinkers. They used to pitch their tents right on the Coup, and I used to feel sorry for them because some of the Coup was smelly and they were there in all weathers.

I can hear my mother yet. When it was a particularly stormy or snowy night and she had come through the room to see if we were settled for the night, as she tucked us in she'd say: 'Think o' they puir tinkers oot on the Coup. Are you no lucky?'

Still to this day, if the weather outside is awful I hear her words in my mind, and I think about the tinkers, wherever they are.

However, they were not so popular in our street when one old man used to just turn up and start playing his bagpipes for money, or sugar and tea. If the bairn had just been put down to sleep and the next minute his bagpipes skirled my mother would mutter, 'If Eh go oot there ee'll be eatin they bagpipes.'

Then a disembodied voice from an open window would ask him to please be quiet, but not exactly in those words. And his pal got the same when he came along too.

Then the old man's pal would go round into the back green and sing up at the windows, and he was rubbish! He couldn't sing a note. Even as a kid I knew he was the pits. Once again my mother's offering on 'Caruso' (that's what she christened him and we all called him that): 'Eh think he gets a copper threw oot o' ane o' the windies right away jist tae shut him up. Heez's no daft, eh?'

None the less when they came to our door my mother would nearly always give them a copper or two, and always fill their tea cans and give them a roll or a slice of bread with whatever she had on it.

The old man usually just sat on our doorstep, but if the weather was cold he would sit up the outside close that ran parallel with our house. And it was there that I would go and have a crack with him. He had a plaidie and a Tam-o'-Shanter bunnet which I thought were great. My mother would repeatedly pull me back if he was up the close and I was making for out the door hissing:

'Dinna tak anything oot o' eez bag tae eat. Dinna ask fir a len o' eez hat or eez shawl. And definitely dinna sit next tae eez doag.'

So with all that in mind I'd just hunker across from him and pass the time of day. I did 'clap eez doag' though, but only if no one was watching.

Other tinkers, mainly women and kids, used to come round and try to get money or food for telling fortunes, or selling wee odds and ends. Oh! And lucky white heather. 'No very bliddy lucky fir them, wiz it?' was one of my grandmother's offerings on it all.

One of the tinkers had a horse and a wee covered cart, and a big wheel he peddled with his foot that sharpened all the knives and cutlery. But that horse would've never gotten a part in a Tom Mix movie I can tell you.

If my memory serves me, a couple of times I was along the Ninewells having a walk with my father and we met some prisoners of war. I believe they were Italians, and must have been barracked near Dundee, because they used to be out digging near Kingoodie Quarry. He would sometimes stop and have a wee blether with them, but I guess they weren't there for long, because the war was over by 1945, so they would all be sent home.

Then there was the excitement of the carnival when it came

to Dundee, it was nearly always 'doon at the Meddlie'. The carnival wasn't nearly so sophisticated back then, but many a happy hour I spent at the weekend getting whirled and birled and then feeling sick.

In the winter, we used to go down to the Meddlie with our sledge, which was painted green and had 'Southern Cross' written in white along the edges, with huge metal runners that just glided along the snowy grass. It held at least four of us; seven if it was a pillie-up.

One really important gathering that went on 'doon beh the wahter' in Dundee for many years was the Monkey's Parade.

Years later, when I joined in the new Monkey's Parade, it had changed location from the river side to the old Overgate, but my mother told me that the same parade used to be along the Esplanade.

It took place on Sundays. Folk used to walk back and forth along the side of the river, and it was where lads met lasses and vice versa.

So everybody would dress in their Sunday best and parade up and down the street, which is exactly what we did in the Overgate and for exactly the same reasons.

I have yet to get an explanation of why it was called the 'Monkey's Parade'.

Anyway, this ritual only ceased in the late 50s or early 60s.

Yup! Happy times on Sundays doon beh the wahter.

* * *

I recall as an adult hearing that they were knocking down my old tenement as part of a re-development of the area.

Most of the 'Sunday alang the wahter' stuff had been vanishing as well: the old swimming baths; the swimming

12

huts on the Esplanade; the old football pitches; the Fifies. Lots of the Coup had been reclaimed, as had Kingoodie Quarry.

Dundee had moved on (quite rightly so) and was now about to build what has turned out to be a completely new West End, apart from a few landmarks like the Whitehall Theatre. There were eventually to be new university blocks and halls, and student accommodation. But most of that was still in the future.

My father would have been well pleased that a university was built there.

Soon after I knew it was all coming down, I went back to spend one last Sunday up the West End, and 'doon beh the wahter'.

I wandered along the cul-de-sac where I was brought up, and it was just a tiny wee square, but this was the road I used to fly along from school.

The houses were tiny, cramped and dead.

I scrubbed at one of the window panes of my grand-mother's place with a paper tissue and peered in. What a mess. And the old mill wall, with its dilapidated scruffy bricks that joined onto her house, only added to the feeling of dilapidation.

The mill stack alone looked in good repair and is still there to this day; it's protected. I stood looking up at it and wondered how many countless folk had passed through the doors of the mill it had shadowed, and here it was . . . a brick chimney, that was being protected.

I tried to go up the closie so I could see my beloved back greenie but it looked like it could fall into rubble any minute so I gave that a miss. I did manage to see it from another vantage point as I left, and the back greenie was no bigger than a postage stamp.

The campsite must've been taken up by just one wee blanket tent. The back greenie pehrtys would only hold a few chairs. The greenie poles we swung on were only feet apart.

I wiped away some of the dirt from our window and peered through that as well. It was just as much a mess, but I decided I was going to go in if I could. So I shoved on the front door of my house until I got it open.

I stood in the two feet by two feet wee 'loaby'. The coat hangers were gone from the walls and the back of the door. The wood on the loaby press was all cracked and rotten.

I pushed open the kitchen door. There were wine bottles, old papers, old blankets and just a whole load of old rubbish scattered all over the place. So it had had some occupants not too long before. I couldn't see the wee black sink, or the jaw box that had one cold-water brass tap.

My mother would have had a fit if she'd seen her wooden bunker, window sills and doorstep. In fact, she'd have had a double fit if she'd seen the whole place.

But what struck me most and will remain with me forever is how small and cramped the place was. We used to have beds, furniture, clothes, other household goods, but for the life of me I couldn't figure out where she'd hidden them all.

I glanced at the alcove where my parents' bed used to be, and imagined my infant sister as she slept in the wicker washing basket at the foot of the bed.

I couldn't get ben-the-room, there was too much rubble in the way, and I couldn't get up the closie, so I just rifled around until I got a slate from the grate, wiped it down, put it in my hand bag and left.

I walked down to the Meddlie and made a point of going to my mother's seat just opposite the bandstand. As I sat, I looked down at the dipped worn old path that had been marked in front of the bench by the many feet that had sat there. I will be forever amazed at the strength and fortitude of my parents' generation.

And so, once again, I spent time simply being 'doon beh the wahter.'

And I enjoyed it just as much as ever.

# THE WORLD O'
# THE WASHIE

When I was young, communal public wash houses were an integral part of tenement life. Most areas in Dundee had their own 'washie'. These establishments were run and maintained by the local councils. My mother went to Miller's Wynd Washie, up the West End of the City. I always think that sounds very grand – The West End – it was a normal working-class area of its time.

Due to the size of the families back then, most Dundonian women spent a great deal of time in these places. My own mother was there at least three times a week, often four times. Therefore, an essential piece of equipment for most of the houses in the tenements was a child's old pushchair, known as a 'washie-tannie'.

After they had served their time as baby carriages, washie-tannies were relegated to carrying the laundry to and from the steamie. They were usually one of your own, or gifted to you after the owner had done with it. They could also be bought from the 'raggies' [second-hand shops]. Raggies did a roaring trade in old Tansads for use in the washing houses. However, my own mother had five kids and sisters and brothers, so she always had a supply of old Tansads on hand. I remember one time thinking what a toff I was when my mother bought a

Tansad from the raggie and it had chrome handles and wheels. I couldn't wait to get to the wash house to meet my pals there.

The real beauty of a Tansad was that once it had finished with its baby-minding duties, it just rolled into its other labours without even having to be adjusted. And washie-tannies were used for much, much, more than just lugging the dirty washing to the wash house.

Whilst my mother was doing the washing, our washie-tannie could be turned into a tank, a chariot, a racing car, a stage coach, a train and a bus, to name but a few.

When the chassis was knackered you were left with a perfect set of wheels for a piler. This provided a helpie-up seat for your wee brother or sister, meaning you didn't have to pull their arms out of their sockets as you dragged them about with you, and prevented you having to listen to them girnnin: 'Eh'm tired, Eh wahnt up.'

But mostly a washie-tannie came into its own when it was being used as just that.

I have watched as my mother piled up her metal wash basket with the blankets and sheets then shoved another load of washing on top of all that. She would stick the scrubbing board, Oxydol, fairy soap and a bottle of Parazone, down the sides of the tannie. Finally, she would tie the lot together with a rope and then wind the rope round the handle to make it all secure.

I recall my brother, who was perhaps aged two at the time, being hoisted up onto the top of this cloth multi-storey. My mother would keep one hand on him and off we'd go, him with both hands firmly gripped onto the tannie's handle, just like you drive your car, only I bet he was having more fun.

I used to trot alongside with my own wee pram filled with my own washing. My mother would put some of the dirty socks in an old pillow case ('washie-bag' to me), and I'd walk along beside her to the washie to 'get meh washin done'.

When we arrived at our washie you paid to get in at the front desk. The front desk consisted of a wee bollie (desk with a window usually) where you pushed the money through and the woman issued you a receipt with your cubicle number on it.

The cubicle was like a four foot by four foot open cell. It had metal walls and a wrought-iron door. It housed two huge sinks, a draining board, a metal boiler that was heated by a gas light from underneath, a dry board for sorting out the clothes, and a long wooden slatted board to stand on at the sinks. This board allowed the water to drip through and run down the open ducts that wound their way through all the stalls in the washie. You know, I never found out where that water ended up. Back in washie world I suppose.

All the women hung their coats over the gates when they were working, and most women wore rubber aprons and tied their hair up with a head scarf. When I went to the washie with my mother I always wore my head scarf too, for she let me 'help' her, if I wanted to. She would fill the boiler first and get all that going, and then if I was helping, she would fill up a sink for me and stick over another box so that I could reach the sink. Apparently, when I was a kid, I was a great wee washer. I do remember that I loved being up to the elbows in the soapy bubbles with one of my mother's old rubber aprons tied under my armpits.

There were huge communal iron spinners ('squeezers' to us). They were operated by belts that went from the back of the machines round a wheel, and I can tell you they went at some rate. My mother used to throw the washing in and, when it was done, she'd throw her weight on the metal pedal at the base of the spinner, bringing it to a shrieking halt.

There were also massive communal boilers and mangles for doing 'big washins' such as blankets and sheets. I'd play swings on the iron wheel handles of the huge mangles that were in the ironing room of the washie. These mangles could almost press a sheet with one turn through. Many's the sweat I've worked up turning that wheelie on the end of the mangle when I got a bit bigger. And I wish I'd a fiver for every blanket or sheet I shook or folded with my mother in that Miller's Wynd Washie.

Last – but by no means least – there were the 'horses'. John Wayne never had a horse as powerful as the ones they had in my washie! The huge iron horses were lined like sentinels along the bottom wall of the washie, situated over the boiler room pipes so that the heat travelled up and dried the clothes.

Sitting along the wall beside these magnificent iron free-standing pulleys were the long metal poles that my mother used to fish her items of washing back up from the boiler room below if they fell off the horse. If she couldn't reach them then the man who swept the floors had to come and do it for her. It was a real bummer if it was a sheet that hadn't been anchored properly because, of course, the item had to be washed all over again.

One horse was allocated per stall. If your stall was number twelve, then you used the corresponding pulley. The tannie was used to humph the washing to and from the huge metal clothes spinners, and then to where the big metal clothes horses were, so that you could hang up your washing. But, as usual, folk had more clothes than clothes horses. This was always causing trouble, especially at high days and holidays like Christmas and New Year.

As soon as we arrived in the washie my mother would organise all the stuff, hastily wash one item, then turn and say to me: 'Hurry up an pit this wet shirt on number ten horse (this was, of course, *not* the number we had been allocated). An stand guard till Eh get doon, an only tak it aff an run back here weh it if the wifie whaz horse it is goes for the biler-man.'

So off I'd scurry, keeping watch to see no one was paying any attention to me. I'd sling the wet shirt over the stolen horse any old how, then sit back a short distance from the horses and stand sentinel duty.

If the place was busy, you could bet your bottom dollar that the next thing, who would appear but the true owner of horse number ten. She'd open up the horse, see the shirt, then turn round and demand from the world at large: 'Wha'z booked this horse? It's meh horse.'

On receiving no reply, she'd get louder and, eventually, if she couldn't steal someone else's horse, she'd turn with a 'Well . . . Eh'm certainly no plahzed at this caper' look on her face and demand for a final time, 'WHAZ ON THIS HORSE?'

By this time everyone in the vicinity would be declaring that it's wasn't them, and that: 'Some fowk dinna gie a monkey (or words to that effect), an they should ken better, wha-iver it is. Abody hiz thir ain washin, an needs thir ain horse.'

I can remember sitting there watching it all, and silently thinking, 'Yeh. Like they never stole anybody else's horse, an Eh don't think!'

By then Mrs Hizzna-got-a-horse would be getting really wound up: 'Right then, that's it! Eh'm aff fir Wullie/ Peter/Boab (whoever the boiler-man happened to be who was on that shift).' And off she'd stomp.

I would grab my chance. Excitement over, everybody was going back to doing whatever they were doing before the fun began. I'd whip the offending article off the horse, praying there still wasn't a straggler lurking, then run back to my cubicle and report.

'Eh kept it as lang as Eh could, but she went aff on a tangent fir the biler-mannie.'

My mother's usual philosophical reply was, 'Och well! Niver mind. Yeh couldna dae any mair than yeh've done.'

It took me until I was an adult myself to get the logic of the fact that my mother used to go for the boiler-man in high dudgeon herself if someone stole her horse, but quite happily nicked someone else's if she could get away with it.

No wonder kids get confused!

It was also highly rumoured where I lived that many a boiler-man picked his spot on the Tay Rail Bridge over the Christmas and New Year holidays when everybody needed at least three horses.

One afternoon recently, as I was sitting on the bus, a young woman came on with her baby in this very swanky pushchair. It was lovely. It had two smaller back wheels and a big wheel in the front. It looked great.

Suddenly, from inside me, I heard my mother's voice as she said:

'Meh Goad. I'd've never gotten meh washin ontae that skinny wee thing.'

And I joined in by thinking: 'Yeh, an it wid mak a rotten cartie.'

Funny how some things stay with you forever.

# MAIR WASHIE WEYS

I have a feeling that 'washies' keep cropping up in other chapters of this book.

When I thought about why this would be, I realised how much a part of my life that building was at that time. For just as you take your kids to McDonald's now, my mother used to trail us to the washie with her when we were wee, or off school, just like most of the women she knew there did, so we'd always company.

Public Wash Houses provided much, much more, than just a means by which you could keep your clothes clean. They were used to wash everybody's hair or the kids for school the next day; as meeting places, confessionals, counselling and therapy suites; for a good blether with your pals, or morale boosters when you were low; as free child-minding services and wailing walls.

They were places for all the women to agree 'well, that's men fir yeh', while the kids played chasies round the steamie with the washie-tannies to the multi-voiced warnings of:

'Dinna run!! Yeh'll slup in the wahter.'

'Whaur's your mither, till Eh tell her on yeh.'

'Here's the biler-man, yeh'r fir it now!'

The boiler-man, lord of all he surveyed; the ticket wifie,

who was also the person who sold single portions of washing powder, bleach and soap, if you hadn't brought your own, or couldn't afford a whole packet of powder or a whole bottle of bleach; the mechanic, he who must be obeyed, at least when he was looking, if you wanted the machines to work; and the 'auld mannie' that slooshed out the stalls at regular intervals, and who was a dead shot with that sweeping brush if you got on his nerves too much. They're all still here in my mind right enough.

We played amongst the stalls, the wringers, the spinners, and as kids we just had a ball. We didn't have many safety procedures or rules in those days, but we had one major rule.

When in the washie you obeyed your mother, your grannie, your auntie, your mother's washie pals, the rest of the women there, the boiler man, the sweeper-upper, the woman at the cash desk, and old Uncle Tom Cobbley if he appeared. But apart from that there were, as I said, no rules.

One of the great beauties of the washie for us as kids was that you could run about in your wellies and splash water to your heart's content. And for kids that lived upstairs in a tene-ment (I lived in the low door), they could thunder around the place as much as they liked, without getting the brush down-stairs thumped on the ceiling.

However, the general freedom of the washie led to some close calls. I had at least two near squeaks with the huge mangles that were housed in an adjacent room. One day, as I swung on the handles, I decided to put my fingers between the rollers. They should've had me at the walls of Jericho; it would have been down in a flash!

Later that day, after it was ascertained that I had neither lost nor broken any fingers, I was rushed to the privacy of my own washing cubicle to be shaken (and stirred) by she who must be obeyed.

My mother told me, in no uncertain terms, that if I ever caused any upset like that again (bear in mind I'm getting this while my fingers are throbbing away like tom-toms), I'd get something to really scream about.

That statement almost matched up to her well known: 'Yeh must like getting a thick ear, dae yeh?' after she'd dealt with some demeanor on my part.

One of the best bits about the washie was piecey-time. After the day's work was done, my mother used to have a cup of tea with her washie pals. That was when the biscuits and tea appeared. The flask and the biscuits were something else that was shoved into the tannie before we left our house. And I got to sit in the tannie and have a rest from running around like a headless chicken.

Oh! And I loved the freezing cold water that you got to drink in the washie. I used to get a drink out of a metal bowl with a wooden handle that we called a 'washie-pannie' (I think that's as in 'pannier' for those of you who lived in Broughty Ferry).

In my mind, I feel the click of the metal pannier on my teeth and feel the cold rim with my lips. I taste the water as it trickles over my teeth and down my throat and makes me feel good. I see my mother's hands as she holds the metal bowl for me and tilts it. Her hands are still pink and washie-wrinkled. Sometimes, she gives me a drink from her hands if she's not up to the armpits in soapy suds, and I love that even better.

I smell her now as if she's standing next to me. She smells like the sheets we fold; the towels; the clean nappies; her rubber apron; getting into bed in between the clean sheets.

But most of all, I hear her as I gulp down the cold water. She is cracking our usual piecey-time joke: 'Jeezy-peeps, slow doon. If yeh drink much mair, yeh'll pee yehr breeks, an then Eh'll hae tae start the washin a ower again.'

Then we both laugh . . . every time.

On washie days, stuffed down the side of her Tansad, along with everything else, my mother would have a shift of underwear for us as well.

Part of our routine was for us to go along to Millers Wynd with her (or meet her there if we were at school), and get washed, and put a clean set of underwear on. This saved us having to wash in the wee black sink at home and she had less dirty washing the next time.

My mother would hang her coat over the door and we'd strip, have a wash, get our hair washed with that exotic carbolic soap, and then a new shift of underwear.

Carbolic soap (that soft green bar with the baby in its nappy stamped on it) did everything when I was a kid. It washed the clothes, it washed your hair, and it washed yourself.

The exceptions to this were: the baby; if you were going someplace special, like someone's party; or something at the school. Then, you could use the Pears soap that you could see right through and smelled really nice.

All the scrubbin-an-a-rubbin duly done and dusted, off we'd go to enjoy the delights of playing in our own 'Washie-Water-World'. Just like Disney World, but no whales or dolphins.

And here's something else. Attached to our Washie was an actual Public Bath House, which we used as well.

We used to meet my father on Wednesday and Friday when he came home from his work as an electrician with the Caledon Shipyard, known to everyone as simply 'The Yaird'.

The Bath House consisted of a huge white and green tiled room, which housed about ten (or maybe more) bathrooms. There was, of course, a roof on the building, but there were no roofs on the actual bathrooms, but walls and a door.

There were two types of bathrooms. Bathroom one had a sink and a bath, with tiled floors and a wooden seat and bath mat. It had two taps, but only one tap which was operated by the occupier of this bathroom, and this tap provided only cold water.

The hot water was provided by the 'bath-mannie', who had control of the hot water from outside the bathroom. He let the hot water into the bath for you, and then you just topped up with cold yourself.

Bathroom two was identical to bathroom one apart from the fact that both taps worked in bathroom two, and you could have as much hot water as you wanted. But, of course, this bathroom was more expensive. I cannot remember the costs offhand now, but I think number one was a shilling and number two was one shilling and thruppence.

When we went with my father to the bath house he always had a posh bath, so that we could get lots of hot water. But he would then ask the man if we could all share the bathroom. So my father would go in and have his bath first, then us kids would go in and all have our bath.

He never got refused, although the bath man probably would have been in hot water (pardon the pun but I couldn't resist it) if he'd been found out, and he used to say: 'Well, dinna yaze up too much hot water then, an dinna tak fir ever.'

This was not an uncommon practice at all back then, and the wonder of it all was how spotlessly clean my folk did keep all of us, without a wardrobe full of clothes, 101 lotions and potions, fancy washing machines and three showers a day. Absolutely more credit to them for looking after us so well!

Anyway, family legend has it that when we were allocated 'oor new hoose' in Fintry housing scheme and my father went to the bath house for his 'final Friday dook' before we had our very own bathroom, he told the old man in charge he'd got a brand new house and that we wouldn't be coming back, to which the man replied: 'Well, the water rates up this end o' the toon are bound tae come doon. Fir Eh've never kent sae mony fowk that could hae a wash fir one an three!'

But then all things are relative.

In later years, as we all grew up, I can remember my father yelling at us when he couldn't get into the bathroom: 'Eh'd hae a better bliddy chance o' gettin intae a bathroom back at the washie!'

# 'SHOUT WHEN YEHR
LEGS GET HOT'

I bet not many people can say that their grannie tried to boil them alive, and she wasn't even the witch from *Hansel and Gretel*.

My grandmother used to do most of her washing in the washing house that sat at the end of the drying green.

The drying green was just for the low door tenants, as the upstairs tenants had the greenie ropes that straddled from the building across to the back of the drying green where there was this huge totem pole that all the ropes were attached to.

The back greenie washie, as opposed to the real washie, was just a single-roomed brick shed. It had two huge white sinks, a wringer and a copper boiler. The copper boiler was built into a brick casing. The copper pot sat in the middle of this and the boiler sat in the corner of the room. It was operated by fire. And it did always remind me of the story of *Hansel and Gretel*.

My grannie would put her sticks under the copper boiler by opening the wee iron gate. It was just like putting the sticks into a kiln. Then she'd fill the boiler with cold water (no hot water heaters then). If the washie had a hose she'd use that and fill up the boiler. If not, then she used to use a metal pannier, known to all in my neck of the woods as a 'washie-pannie'.

She left the first of the water to get hot, then returned and transferred the hot water from the boiler back into one of the two big white sinks. She'd then lift out the clothes for hand washing from the washie-pannie (I would love to know why Dundonians always add 'ie' to the end of lots of words).

Anyway, the next load of cold water would be put in the boiler and so on, until the washing was done.

Now, when she was going to wash the blankets, that needed a whole lot of cold water. She'd fill up the boiler, and then one of the big sinks, and then if I was handy she'd ask, 'Dae yeh want tae tramp in the sink fir iz?'

The water would be tepid, maybe even just luke-warm when she put me in. She'd stick my clothes into my knickers, then instruct as she humphed the hot water over, 'Shout when yerh legs get hot!'

This from a woman who could have put her hands into water that 'wid've bilte an egg', she'd put in so many years of rubbing and scrubbing.

However, I wasn't so daft! I used to start skirling from the word go, 'Eh'm hot, an it's gettin' really burnin' in here. Get me oot! Get me oot!!'

I started this performance about two seconds after I got put in. Eventually her nerves could stand no more. She'd wheech me out with a:

'Oh! Fir Goads sake yeh'd think a murder wiz bein committed. Eh'll dae it mehsel, Greetin Teenie. Yehr mair bahther than it wiz a worth.'

'Daen it ehrsel' only meant that she used the stick that looked like a cudgel and just jabbed away at the blankets until they were clean.

Tenement washing houses served all the folk in the tenement, but everybody had an allotted 'drying day'. Drying days were sometimes a great source of entertainment for me. Us kids, if we were playing in the area, used to gather round and wait for the fun when we heard the battle cry of, 'Wha the hell's pit thir washin oot on meh day?'

This signified that the woman whose day it was to use the greenie had had her turn usurped by someone else.

There was no excuse for this apart from the fact that the other washer was 'chancin her mitt!' and had been found out.

What ensued was the woman whose real turn it was would then tramp round the tenement to find out who had stolen her turn, and 'deal weh her'! That usually meant words of some sort, which usually ended with the stealer-of-turns dragging her washing off the ropes and storming off with a, 'jist wait until you're stuck. Eh jist hope an pray it's on meh day!'

The folk up the stairs who had the outside washing lines all attached to one huge greenie pole used to pile huge loads of washing onto these ropes.

Sometimes you would look up and it was like it was some kind of a celebration with all the clothes fluttering away.

Then the rain would come on.

I once heard a comedian say on television, what is it about us that when it rains we all have to run and get inside, apart from the obvious answer? You would have to be out in a deluge for at least half an hour before you were really soaked. But he was right. The minutes it rained all you could hear around my tenement was: 'Jessie (Mary, Agnes . . . whoever) RUN tell (Mrs A, B, C . . . whoever) that it's rehnin, an the clathes are a gettin weet.'

Then in the next ten minutes, all hell broke loose in Washie World!

There would be the screeching of pullies being dragged in as the owners rescued their clothes.

If my own mother had clothes out I'd run with her and take

armfuls of clothes and bung them in the ben-the-room-windie (we lived on the bottom remember). Then after we'd success-fully saved the washing from being torn to shreds by the rain (even though it was only a threatening drizzle), my mother would dash back up the closie to 'hing the washin on the sticks'; the sticks being a wooden pulley that hung from the roof of the room. We also had 'sticks' that went up in front of the fire. My last job was to pick up the clothes pegs that had been scattered all over the green as we frantically dived about like demented forkies.

I recall asking her once why there was all this running, and she replied: 'Rehns dirty water, an the last thing Eh wahnt is mair dirty washin'. Fair enough! But I never ventured into the logic that when it rained she never thought of the fact that we never got dirty.

But then again when it rained (and after she'd seen to the washing if it was out) she did used to come to the door and yell for us:

'Come. NOW. HURRY. Dae yeh no see it's rehnin, an yeh'll get weet?' Thus depriving us of the one thing we did want to do when it rained.

Oh! That statement reminds me of one of her favourites when we were not doing what we were told:

'Come ower here.'

You did not, of course, move one inch.

'Eh'm speakin tae you.'

You got that all right!

'Eh'm tellin you if yeh dinna come ower here – now! – an Eh hae tae come fir yeh, then yeh'r really fir it. Is that what yeh want?'

Not really, Mother, sprang to mind, but not to mouth. Young as I was I wanted to see my next birthday.

'Right then. Last chance, an then yeh'll be sorry.'

I usually already was. And nine times out of ten that was when I took off like a whippet, knowing that by the time I returned all would be well.

On the other hand my father could stop me at thirty paces just by a look.

Back to the greenie!

If a pulley line snapped off the main pole, and you were lucky enough to be around when it got fixed you could watch the show from the safety of the ground.

The man of that house (remember he could live four storeys up) would have to climb the pole to attach another wheel to hold the rope, or pay someone else a couple of bob to do it for him. I bet the folk on the top of the tenement prayed for no pulley-snapping.

Our low door greenie poles were used for many a thing apart from hanging out washings. One use for our poles, during the school holidays, was to throw old blankets over the ropes and pretend we were away camping.

This only happened, of course, weather permitting, and as we live in Scotland it wasn't all that often that we got to camp out 'all night'.

Camping out all night to us was to wait until after teatime, then depart to go into our tent. 'Us' was usually my older brother and me, and some pals from the tenement.

The mothers would make up food parcels for us. Since we were to be all of ten to twenty feet from the stairs to the building, and in our case eight feet from the ben-the-hoose window, we were certain to be in need of extra sustenance.

And so we set off for the great outdoors of the 'Backies'.

After the novelty of being far from home wore off, we would annoy our parents by knocking on the window and asking for: 'Anither comic. Weh've swapped an rehd them a.' (We read by torch.)

'Anither jumper, Eh'm frozen.'

'Mair water in the lemonade bottle.' (We'd drunk all the lemonade five minutes after we got into the blanket-tent.)

'Somthin else tae eat.'

'Eh need meh pixie (a woollen hat which tied underneath my chin). Meh heid's cauld jist like yeh sade it wid be.'

My mother would take just so much of this, then would inform us that the camping trip was over if she so much as heard another peep.

Round about eight or nine o'clock that same night, my father would come out and help us to dismantle the campsite and we would all go home having convinced ourselves we were now seasoned outdoors-men, having killed a bear if one was unlucky enough to have chanced upon the greenie. More often than not it was a hapless cat that had come over to see who was invading its territory, then got chased for its life.

In a tenement that housed at least twenty families the 'greenie' was part of my playground.

It was used for much more than its purpose, and was the arena for many events in my young life.

# THE POSH KILTIE WEDDIN

We were going to a 'Posh Wedding'. It was to be in the church and then on to a swanky hotel in Carnoustie no less, so this was a 'BIG DO'.

I was about seven years of age.

The preparations for this wedding started weeks and weeks before hand, and the time between the preparations and the wedding were peppered by comments from my father such as, 'Thir wizna this much organisin fir the D-Day rescues,' or 'Wha gies a bugger what goes weh what? Thir's bairns stervin a ower the world,' etc. etc. etc.

My mother was oblivious. We were all to be suited out in style for this wedding and that was that! And so the wedding planner began her own campaign.

We'd all to be kitted out from bottom up: new underwear (in case we got hit with the proverbial bus and as we lay in a pool of blood some wifie would remark, 'Look at that bairn's auld underwear'), new socks, maybe not new shoes for everybody, but new outfits certainly.

And my mother got a whole new outfit. Her outfit has long gone from my memory, but the hat the bag and the shoes will remain forever. The hat was a wee black velvet lily with a veil that had black spots on it. The bag was velvet too, and she had a rose spray pinned to it. The shoes were black suede high heels with bows, and were sling backs.

I remember thinking that they were just like the film stars wore in the films, but when my mother was all 'dolled up' for that wedding she looked better than any of them.

However, I bet on the day of a wedding none of them would have landed up shaking their kid like a rabbit, because of a simple accident that could have happened to anybody.

The week before the wedding all the new attire was ready and hanging in the wardrobe; the taxi was booked and the flowers were ordered.

Then the day of the wedding arrived.

There was a frenzy of hair washing and getting ready. As I recall the day, it strikes me that it must have been some melee, us all getting ready in two small rooms, and that's another reason for what happened not long before the taxi was due.

Because the house was so small, when we were going to any occasion, my mother got us ready systematically. She saw to us first and then she and my father got ready last.

So, after my mother had got my older brother and myself ready, she sent us to stand outside with the usual instructions once you were cleaned and ready to go:

'Dinna move fae that door. Dinna dare play aboot an get dirty. Dinna scuff yehr shoes. Jist bide oot the road an wait fir the taxi.'

So there we stood. Me all dolled up in my new blouse and red kilt, and flower proudly pinned through my blouse and onto my vest, and a shine on my shoes that nearly called for sunglasses, escorted by my brother and him all spit and polish as well.

We stood there for what seemed to us a lifetime, and then my brother said, 'Eh think it wid be ok if weh jist went up the closie and stood in the back greenie.'

Since lots of our disasters began with great ideas from my brother I often wonder why I never questioned that 'this time' anything would be different.

So off we went.

Memory does not serve me as to what started the dispute between us, but then that never mattered much anyway. What did matter was that when my brother shoved me I fell up against the stone wall at the side of the back green where there was a huge nail sticking out, and proceeded to rip half the side of my kilt away.

We both stood there, suspended in disbelief, as my white knickers appeared through the gaping hole in the kilt like the moon shining through some waving standard on a battle-field.

My brother looked at my terror stricken face.

'It's no as bad as it looks.' Yeh! Right!

I belted back down the close and shouted through the door: 'Thirs been a wee accident, an Eh've tore meh kilt.'

She appeared like a cannonball.

What followed were shrieks of, 'Tore yehr kilt; get ower here. Oh! Meh Goad, look at the mess o' yeh. If yeh werna dressed fir this weddin Eh'd murder yeh.'

What spared me from this fate was the fact that the taxi would be appearing very soon. So I was rushed inside and my mother mended the kilt as best she could, muttering: 'Eh might hae kent better than let yeh oot meh sight. An look at how squint the side o' yehr new kilt is now.'

However, my saviour, the taxi, appeared and we all set out for a day when I remember thinking the bride looked like a princess, the steak pie was wonderful, the trifle was even more wonderful, and my flower lasted most of the day before it wilted and dropped off the safety pin.

We did get our photograph taken, and you know what? I bet nobody looking at that photograph even noticed the wavy line down the side of my kilt.

# WORLD WAR II AN THE GLESKAE HOLIDAY

I was born approximately seven months after World War II began.

At that time, my father was an electrician in the Caledon shipyard (The Yaird) in Dundee, and he was sometimes sent through to the shipyard in Govan to work during the war.

He worked with teams of men they called 'Black Squads', although I have no explanation for this name. But they were there to fix up the boats and submarines that came in for repair.

I remember him recalling, years later, that they got something like £3.00 a time; I think it was for testing the electrics on a submarine. For that, they sailed the ship out into the Clyde, down into the water, tests were carried out and back up it came. Then he got paid some of his wages in war-bonds, and never got the real money until much later on.

I have no personal recollections of the war apart from starting school, and carrying my gas mask with me that I thought had a Mickey Mouse face. Then we would get instructions as to what to do if there was any danger of us getting bombed, and that was to get below the desks. But I wasn't at the school all that long when the war ended.

My war memories are more about the shortages after the

war; about eating dried eggs because the real ones were rationed, as were lots of goods. Anyway, I loved that dried egg. It was just like a pancake.

I remember queuing up at the butchers (and other shops) with my mother. And if a shop got an item in that was scarce, then the word went round like wildfire, and the queue was a mile long before you could say Jeck Roabson.

Him again! That man must've been the equivalent to Dundee's Roger Bannister because his name was used to fit any occasion when she wanted us to move quicker:

'Hurry up an weh'll be hame afore yeh kin say Jeck Roabson.'

'Get yehr shoes on. Eh wahnt tae get there afore yeh kin say Jeck Roabson.'

Or, in the case of telling her my gloves were soaking and my hands were freezing on one winter's day:

'Bla on them. Weh'll be hame afore yeh kin say Jeck Roabson.'

So I'm sure, no matter what the queue, Jeck Roabson was at the head of it every time.

Another thing, when the baker got cakes in he would allocate between two and four cakes, or pastries, or buns etc. per customer, depending on how much bakery goods he received that particular day.

It was not uncommon practice for a woman to put her kids in one part of the queue and stand in another part herself, thus getting the goodies they required. But the baker, and anyone else who found out about this covert action, weren't too happy (although they were all at it I imagine), and the woman who had been found out would be told in no uncertain terms what was thought of her doing this.

I remember my mother telling me that one day she went along to the bakers because she was getting visitors. As she needed the extra bakery, she decided to sneak my older brother in the queue ahead of her. She was his mother and had known him all his life, so she should have known better, I think!

Anyway, he apparently was instructed to get 'twa cat's faces (also known in other parts of Dundee as 'pigs' fuhts') or 'twa sair heids'. A translation of which is: two flaky pastries with icing on the top that were shaped to appear like cats' ears (or pigs' trotters), and a small round Madeira cake with icing on the top, which had a greaseproof paper wrapping circling its circumference, thus making it appear to be a bandaged wounded head. And yes it does indeed lose something in the translation!

Anyway, the bold boy duly got up the queue and into the shop. Two seconds later he reappeared and yelled down the queue at the top of his voice:

'Ma! Thiv nae cat's faces left, an thiv nae sair heids left, so whit are yeh wahntin?'

Then the baker appears behind him:

'Eh! An that's yehr lot Mrs.'

When my mother finished relating this story ending with:

'That laddie wid've got yeh hung, whit a rehd face.'

Not for the first time did I ponder that it is no surprise that kids get confused about what their elders do!

Once the war was over and my father didn't have to travel backwards and forwards to Glasgow, his Glaswegian pal he'd met while working there invited us over for a holiday. And we were going to go!

Back then we were well looked after and well cared for, but what is an accepted part of most kids' lives nowadays, like a holiday, was a great excitement to us.

I think it would probably be for a week's stay we went for, but since going away from our own house for more than a night was as yet unknown to me, I thought I was getting a better deal than that guy Aladdin had on his travels after the Genie of the lamp gave him a magic carpet.

So off we went to Glasgow like the Broons setting forth: bairns, bags, baggage, Tansad and all.

We were met at the railway station by my Dad's pal and he took us by bus to where he lived. His wife's mother lived in the same close as them, so there 'wiz plehnty room fir abody'.

I was impressed by their closie. They lived up a *tile* close. Its main colour was white, but it had a green and orangey colour mixture of wee tiles that created a decoration about half way up the walls.

Their actual house had three rooms and an inside toilet.

But the very best of all, as far as I was concerned, was the bed that folded up into a cabinet when it wasn't in use. It sat in the corner of the kitchen and I got to sleep in that. Sure I had a cosy bed back home, but a bed that folded away in a cabinet – it was no contest in my mind!

I can still remember how excited I was about that bed, that I even wanted to go to bed early! I bet my mother thought of buying one there and then.

That first night I can remember lying in that cabinet bed (I shared it with either my brother or sister) pretending it was Dorothy's house from the *Wizard of Oz*. I'd never slept in a wardrobe before. This was indeed a grand start to the 'Gleskae' holiday.

And so we jaunted around Glasgow, or played in the street with our new found 'holiday pals', and I generally loved my very first holiday.

Some afternoons we went to an Italian Ice Cream Parlour where you could get a sit down ice cream treat. (In Dundee we had such a place called 'The Washington' for those of you who are not recycled teenagers like me.)

41

The ice cream parlour walls were all white and blue decorated tiles. The tabletops were white with a blue checked pattern to match the décor, and were made of that heavy washable plastic fabric.

The ice cream shop spoons were like wee silver ladles and fluted at the edges, and the ice cream bowls were silver as well and looked like miniature Grecian urns.

You could have every flavour of ice cream your heart desired. And these could be had with pears, mandarins, pineapple, peaches and real bananas (remember some of us had never seen a banana until after the war, because of their scarcity).

I must've gone on about that silver spoon and bowl so much that the Italian man who owned the shop was pushed into letting me have one, just to shut me up I suppose.

I treasured that spoon and bowl for ages after my holiday, and then it vanished into 'grew oot o' it' world. Yet obviously the memories of them stay with me.

But then I believe you never really lose anyone (or anything) that really matters to you. I believe you can keep them forever.

# BOATYAIRD CHRISTMAS PRESSIES

When my father worked in the boatyard in Dundee some of our Christmas presents came from there, done as 'homers' by the men.

I had a whole 'washie set' made up by one of the joiners. It was a miniature wash tub and stand, a wooden soap dish and a wooden scrubbing board. There was also a wooden dryer for hanging my washing on. I can remember filling the tub up with water and scrubbing away at the socks and hankies for hours, and hanging and re-hanging them on the dryer.

In fact there's a pre-Christmas story about that washing set.

My mother had gone to the pictures one night with her sisters and my father was left in charge, and as he read his papers or book I went through the room to play with my brother.

I was playing hide and seek with my younger brother ben-the-room when I decided that I would move the dressing table (which was in the corner in front of the ben-the-room press). So, little as I was, I shoved away until I got the dressing table moved and room for me to slip into the press (my brother must've been tired of just sitting there with his eyes shut).

As I tried to slip into the cupboard, I found I couldn't get in because it was crammed with this stuff all covered in brown paper.

I opened the parcel.

Joy of Joys! A washing board set and some books and selection boxes.

I tore it open some more. By this time my wee brother had flashed across the room.

'LOOK! LOOK! Santy Klazz hiz come early.' I was over the moon!

So we two happy campers shoved and dragged out the stuff into the middle of the floor. I started playing 'washies', and the two of us proceeded to finish off the contents of the first selection box.

My father must have heard the commotion, and opened the door: 'Whit's a the rack . . . ?'

'Dad, yeh'll niver believe it. Santy Klazz must've came early, sneaked in, and left meh washie set, and a load o' sweeties and books. Ee'll be bringin the rest efter, Eh suppose.'

Did I notice for one nanosecond that my father was just standing there not saying a word (which was not my usual father)? No, I didn't. And when he just closed the door, did I think that's not normal either when you think you're in for a telling off? Nothing was bothering me. 'Santy Klazz hid come early.'

When I think of this, on the real Christmas day I got my usual stocking and stuff, and another gift that wasn't as big as the main one.

My mother explained that Santy Klazz had left my *big* present early so I couldn't expect to get it twice.

If I remember rightly I think I just thought I'd got two big pressies anyway, as I got something else on Christmas day, and I'd had the fun of playing with my 'washie set' for at least some days before Christmas.

We nearly always got a sledge with real metal runners and it was usually big enough to hold the lot of us when we went along to the Magdalene Green to use it.

It was painted green and called the Southern Cross. We had up to a Southern Cross IV which travelled all the way to Fintry with us before we all eventually got too old for sledging.

My brothers would get a wooden fort and soldiers made out of lead. These soldiers were usually Kilties.

But the present that sticks in my mind the most is my doll's house.

I can remember getting up and going through the room and there it was. The most beautiful thing I'd ever seen.

The doll's house was made out of wood and had a hinged wooden roof that you lifted and looked into the four rooms. I remember one of the first things I thought about it was that the dolls had more space than us.

My father had wired up the house with these tiny wee bulbs and there was a switch at the side of the house where you could put the lights off and on.

One of my uncles had made a whole load of rexine (imitation leather) furniture, and my mother had cut up old carpet bits to cover all the floors. That was also more than I had in my own house.

My Auntie Mary had knitted tiny dolls' clothes to fit the two wee dolls that were seated on the settee when I opened the lid.

I remember I just sat and hugged that doll's house the whole day and everybody that came in was shown how the lights went off and on and how the furniture was 'real' and I was chuffed to bits that, 'Santy must've been really lustin fir Eh got jist whit Eh wanted.'

I played with that house until it was old and battered, but

as is the way of life, it vanished to I know not where, and possibly landed up as firewood after the umpteenth kid had enjoyed it.

In the 'Yaird' there were joiners who worked alongside my father, who provided these Christmas presents for us kids. I don't suppose one of them ever knew of the countless happy times one wee lassie had playing with the doll's house he built for her.

I wish now I could have met him.

# CARMEN MIRANDA
# COMES TAE OOR BACK
# GREENIE PEHRTY

Did you ever have a 'back greenie pehrty' during the 'seven weekies' where you lived?

This was tradition in my street when I was a kid.

A day would be selected during the summer holidays when the schools were off, and then everybody heaved to and organised an afternoon's entertainment, which was provided by us kids, and included a great time to be had by everyone.

On the day of the party, some of the women who lived in my tenement would all get together and provide the eats, the furniture and the stage. Costumes had to be provided for you by your own family.

All the kids got dressed up. The blankets were used to make stage curtains by flinging them over the washing ropes. Folk used to bring out chairs and arrange them like a real theatre and got ready for when we 'did wir turn'.

Your turn could be anything: a poem, a story, a dance, a song, some kind of acrobatic feat. I think the latter was created especially for my older brother who, to quote my mother, 'wiz like a flech in a blanket'! So he usually did some jumping-about thing.

Well this particular year I set my heart on going to the

'pehrty' as Carmen Miranda, who was my heroine of the time, even though she had rubber ears!

I had first seen Carmen at the Princess Cinema with my mother and one of my aunties, and I fell in love in an instant. This Brazilian rumba dancer and film star of the 1940s could sing like a linty, dance like she had snake hips, and wore huge high-heeled shoes that glittered.

She had a hat that was about a foot tall and covered in enough fruit and veg to feed five hundred!

I knew right away that I wanted to be Carmen, so I set about learning how. I badgered my mother until she taught me the words of one of the songs from the film, and then tormented anyone who would let me into performing her song-and-dance routine for them. So it would come as no surprise to anybody, I would imagine, that this year Carmen Miranda was coming to our 'do'.

So on the day, one of my aunties perched me up on the bunker and made me up with rouge, lipstick, mascara and eye shadow.

The eye shadow was dark and somehow I see it in my mind as a charcoal colour, which made me look like I'd had a couple of black eyes. Marvellous!

The rouge came out of a wee red box and was powder, which was applied with the end of a hankie, then dusted off!

The lippy was bright red, and my auntie then spat into the wee box that held her mascara and instructed me: 'Mind Now, haud still or yeh'll get yehr eye poked oot!'

That done, she stood me up and put orange-coloured leg tan on my legs, went back to spitting on the wee box of mascara, and then drew lines up the back of my legs for kiddy-on stockings.

They all did this for themselves as well (for real), when they either couldn't get, or couldn't afford, nylon stockings.

She tied an old dishtowel on my head like a turban, pinned a bunch of imitation cherries (taken from a hat I would think) to the turban, and anchored it down with a zillion hair pins to stop it falling (and it didn't).

To finish off, she clipped on some old earrings, put another old cloth or towel round my waist, and I was ready to rock on.

And rock on I did!

I *was* Carmen Miranda the film star, and I tell you, I knew every word and action that woman ever did in that film.

My turn was a song that went something like this:

Aye-Aye-Aye-Aye-Aye . . . I like you very much.

Aye-Aye-Aye-Aye-Aye . . . I think you're grand.

Aye-Aye-Aye-Aye-Aye . . . I really loooooovvvve your touch.

Aye-Aye-Aye-Aye-Aye . . . I beat the band. I beat the band. I beat the band.

Aye-Aye-Aye-Aye-Aye . . . Aye-Aye-Aye-Aye-Aye.

A y e - A y e - A y e - A a a a - h a a a - haahaaaaaaaaaaaaaaaaaaaaaaaaaaaye . . . **AYE!!**

I was a great success, and got rousing applause. In fact, I bet I only left the stage because of a 'GET-AFF' stare from my mother!

And I have to tell you that the 'Aye-Ayes' were absolutely no problem for a kid from Dundee, Scotland, but it was a good job Carmen had rubber ears or she would have heard me knock blue murder out of her accent with the rest of the lyrics.

Yes . . . Carmen Miranda had rubber ears, and her such a good singer as well.

I know because my grannie told me.

One day I'd been harping on while I was practising for

being Carmen. My dishtowel turban kept falling off my head
and I said to my grandmother in frustration:

'Carmen Miranda's turban *niver* fahz aff o' ehr heid when
**she's** singin.'

'That's cause it's peened tae ehr ears.'

'Peened tae ehr ears? But iz that no really really sare?'

'Na . . . she dizzna feel a thing, fir ehr ears are made oot o'
rubber.'

# DAYS OOT

When I was a kid my yearly holiday consisted of 'days oot'.

Actually going to stay in a hotel for any length of time, never mind going on an aeroplane, never even entered our horizons.

Since my father was an electrician who worked in the 'Yaird', any days out were during the 'Dundee fortnight'. But 'days oot' were the norm for everybody where I lived, only the toffs went on aeroplanes.

In those days, practically the whole of Dundee shut down for the holiday fortnight, so that if you went down to the beaches (known to Dundonians one and all as 'The Ferry') then you were sure to know half of the folk that were there.

We lived up the West End of Dundee, so sometimes we would walk along the Perth Road and down to the Sea Breezes, look down at the trains for a while and then walk into town. Sometimes when we finished our 'Day Oot' we would go to the locally famous Deep Sea Fish Restaurant for a 'sit-in chippie tea'.

Once, I remember going through to Glasgow to a pal of my father's and staying there for a whole week, and what a week that was. However, if the weather permitted, and the rain stayed off, we usually landed up at 'The Ferry'.

My mother would get us all up early. My brother and I would run to the grocer for lemonade and crisps, or we just made our own drinks up with a stick of liquorice and water shaken together in an old lemonade bottle and called Sugerellie water.

We had a wee song that we sang as we nearly took our arms out of their sockets shaking away at the concoction. For the Sugerellie to be perfect you'd to sing the song four times, according to who-knows-who, and it went like this:

Sugerellie wahter, black as yehr lum (or yehr bum).
Gether up yehr peens an yeh'll a get some.

I have absolutely no understanding to this day of what that means, but I know my muddy brown drink tasted lovely to me after I'd chanted this rhyme the specified number of times.

My favourite 'pieces' were eggs chopped up in a cup with butter, then spread on bread. The bread wasn't sliced in those days. It had crusty curved tops, which we called 'Curly Kates', and crusty plain bottoms, which we called 'Plehn Geordies'.

All the food, costumes, towels, and the 101 other things necessary for our day at the beach were gathered together. Then all the paraphernalia required for the youngest member of the family, who was still a baby, was hung on the handle of the pushchair. Lastly, we were all allocated our bag to carry. Then, buckets and spades at the ready, we set forth.

We joined the queue at the bus stop in Shore Terrace, along with all the other day-trippers. It always seemed to me then that the queue was a mile long, and that the bus inspector would eventually declare there were not enough buses for everyone.

Then, and this was the unthinkable, we'd have to go home.

It occurs to me now that I only cared about how many buses there were until I got on one, then I waved goodbye quite happily to the folk still waiting, and didn't give a fig if they had to go home.

At last we arrived at the beach and set up our spot for the day.

My mother had a huge black umbrella which she placed over the pushchair. I always thought this was unnecessary as you couldn't see my sister anyway beneath the huge floppy sun hat and all that calamine lotion. She was taken out of the pram and 'aired' from time to time during the day. We were also 'lotioned up' to avoid sunburn. Between our pink bodies and the calamine, we must have looked like wee white ghost dancers.

If it wasn't all that warm we just used to paddle about at the water's edge. I can remember tucking my dress into my knickers and splashing about to my heart's content.

However, if it was really warm then we put on our swimming costumes, or 'dookers' as we knew them, and went mad cavorting about in the waves.

I had a special red woollen swimming costume that my Auntie Mary had knitted for me. I loved that costume, even though it made me itchy in the sun. When it got wet, it magically transformed itself into a skirt, which landed up flapping around about my knees. Did this hinder, or upset me? Not one bit of it!

My beloved wool 'cossie', however, was unceremoniously dumped when I got older, and I became the proud owner of a new posh nylon swimsuit. I imagine the old costume landed up as a cleaning rag.

After our swim we would get dried and changed under a towel changing room, which was held together by my mother. No leaping about in the nude in my days. To quote my mother: 'Wehr no wahn't showin aff a wehr bits fir the world an eez wife tae see, are weh?'

When hunger got the better of us my mother would declare 'piecey-time', and we would all gather round for the food. If it was breezy you'd move to the sand dunes for some protection. And, of course, the wind and the sand were in everything.

My parents had their tea from a thermos flask, while we had our Sugerellie water. This was accompanied by sand-crunchy egg pieces. What Bliss!

This feast was rounded off with some type of goodie or, if my mother had brought some home-made dumpling, we polished that off. Dumpling was definitely my favourite. Sometime during the day, we would get an ice cream cone.

As I recall, my father, like most of the men, just wore his shirt and trousers and his ordinary shoes to the beach. In those days, there was no leisure wear; you were lucky to get any leisure, never mind an outfit to go with it!

At approximately four o'clock in the afternoon we joined the exodus of the homeward-bound heading back to the bus stop. We waited there not too unhappily, because there was one last treat in store. We always finished the day off with a bag of chips to eat outside, on the way home.

Happy Days!

# PALACES AN PICTURES

When I was a kid a night out to the cinema, or as we called it 'the pictures', was very much part of our way of life.

Dundee had many cinemas in those days. In my area alone there were three practically on my doorstep. The Forest Park was up the road, the State (which is now the Whitehall Theatre) was along the road, and my beloved Princess showed films all week, then magically transformed into a cinema club on Saturday mornings.

They changed the programme twice a week, and it was always a double billing. This included a 'B' film we called the 'wee picture'.

First, there was the news with that cockerel crowing all over the place. I never did get that, a bird heralding the news. I used to think they should've used a great big cannon since it was THE NEWS. But perhaps then, like now, folk didn't want to hear the half of it, especially when they were out for a night's enjoyment.

Then there was a trailer of what would be showing the next week, followed by the main film, the interval to get your ice cream or juice, and finally, the wee picture.

So, generally a night at the pictures was exactly that. And there used to be two showings, an early and a late.

You got admitted into the cinema anytime at all. So if you wanted to spend some extra time, you could sit through the whole programme twice, unless the ushers asked to check your ticket to see the time you came in, and then you got turfed out. But that was usually only if there was a queue to get in for the second showing. So folk wandered in and out of the cinema whenever they wished.

If you made too much noise as you tried to find your seat in the dark you were met with:

'Goad's sake sit doon.'

'Shut up that speakin.'

'Hurry up an tak a seat, wehr missin the picture.'

Or other such words of encouragement to invite you to join in the evening's entertainment.

Women were known to carry babes in arms in to the pictures, and had to leave if the kid started crying too loudly.

During the interval between the films you could only buy wee cartons of orange juice, or tubs of Eldorado ice cream that were just in plain white paper, and that was it. They didn't have to waste much money on advertising in the cinemas then; it was take it or leave it.

The usherette who sold the goodies used to walk down the aisle early, and she would shine her torch on the tray she carried, signalling where she would be standing.

Some cinemas had orchestra pits because they had been theatres before being converted. And it was in one of these cinemas that I fell into the pit!

I had been pestering my sister to take me to the toilet in the middle of the film. Now not only did that 'get on abody's goat' that you were disturbing them, it also meant the toilet-taker had to miss some of the film.

I think it must have been about the third time I'd whispered as loud as I could:

'Eh need tae go tae the lavvie.'

'Sheeest,' followed by a glower – again.

I must have persisted until I was attracting too much attention, and then got shoved out to, 'Go yehrsel, an come right back, an nae comin back soakin, weh playin in the sinks.'

So off I trotted, but something interesting must have happened on the screen, and I walked on in the dark whilst watching the film, marched right into the red velvet curtain that hung from the brass rail surrounding the orchestra pit and fell right into the pit.

Well the hullaballo that ensued. I remember yelling at the top of my voice as I rolled down hanging onto the curtain and then I hit the floor (I don't think it was all that steep but it felt like the Law Hill to me).

The picture was stopped. The lights went up. The ushers came running, but were beaten to the spot by my sister who'd heard me screaming. I was hoisted back up. It was ensured that not only were my vocal chords well intact, so was I. I was then frog-marched out of the picture house and dragged all the way home with my sister informing me: 'Eh wull niver, an Eh mean *niver*, tak you tae the pictures again.'

But I'm sure she did.

Oh! And I can remember some of the films were silent when I first started going to the cinema. I absolutely loved Charlie Chaplin, Buster Keaton and all the stars of the silent screen. I laughed with Charlie, and then felt so sorry for him at the end of each film as he wandered away like Nobody's Child. And when Buster Keaton hung from the end of some building by his trouser braces I used to pray the elastic wouldn't give way. That would've been even worse than your knicker elastic snapping, any day of the week.

When it was a silent film and you were sitting beside

anyone who was with an adult (usually their grannie or some other auld body) who couldn't read, then you got pestered the whole night with them reading out loud the words that were written along the bottom of the screen. I was so glad my adults could all read.

If there were a few folk in with someone who couldn't read, (or worse still their grannie was deaf as well as not being able to read) then you were glad the words were written along the bottom of the screen, else you wouldn't have had a clue what was going on with the film for what was going on round about you. And this was at the serious cinema, not the Saturday Club where not hearing, or knowing the plot, never detracted one whit from the entertainment.

Another thing that used to happen in the cinema was that folk felt free to clap and cheer for the hero when he rescued the damsel in distress, and hiss and boo when the wicked landlord was going to throw Little Nell and her grandfather out on the street.

So when Charlie dodged the Keystone Cops, or that tough guy with the stripy shirt and popping eyes, we all hurrahed. When the big bully was after him someone would shout out 'RUN'. And when he hit the bad guys with a pole, we cheered him along.

I grew up with the cinema as one of my main forms of entertainment. To this day I still love 'gaen tae the pictures'.

And I can say the same for the theatre.

My first visit to a proper theatre was to the Palace Theatre. This theatre was situated where the Queen's Hotel car park is now. And many a time the queue to get into the Palace would wind up the brae and round the corner into the street. Many of the shows were sell-outs.

I mainly went to see the singing and dancing shows, with the emphasis on Scottish entertainment. Performers such as

Andy Stewart, Robert Wilson, Will Starr, Johnny Victory, to name a few, were very popular.

My grannie thought Andy Stewart was the best thing since sliced bread, and she never missed going to a performance if it was him.

When I wrote the name Robert Wilson just there, my brain automatically started to sing the first few lines of 'Down in the Glen'.

I never got to see Johnny Victory for, although he was very popular, when I asked if I could go, it was always greeted with, 'No yehr far too wee.' And by the time I wasn't too wee, I didn't 'do' the Palace any more. So to this day I don't know what I missed.

But Will Starr, now he was another story. He played an accordion (I think it was), and sung loads of songs you could sing along with. He used to end some of the songs by giving a wee hooch and kicking his leg to the side.

I was there one time with my grannie and asked her why he did this wee kick thing at the end, and she replied: 'Och, ee canna help it. Eez leg's tied tae the end o' eez accordion weh a lang buttie string, an when ee pulls out eez accordion sideweys, it wheech's eez leg up.'

I never even questioned why he didn't cut the string. I just grew to know better, and to learn that 'pullin meh leg' was just another entertainment for my grannie. But I have to tell you that as a kid I still loved going to see Will Starr.

Even though we all lived in tenements, Scottish entertainment that sung about glens and mountains and 'hearts being in the Highlands', and all that sort of thing, were very popular shows. Yet the only Highlands I ever saw as a kid were the 'Highland Coos' on the bars of toffee. I think we all just loved a good old sing-song.

But the shows I loved at the Palace, really loved, were the pantomimes.

My mother or my grandmother would go to the box office early, book tickets for us (however many 'us' was), pay them up before Christmas week, and then take us to see the pantomime that was on that year.

I remember one Christmas in the middle of the show, when the cast were doing the usual, and inviting kids up on to the stage to join in. This particular pantomime was *Robinson Crusoe* and you were being asked up onto the stage to be boiled alive by the cannibals.

There was this huge pot on the stage and the cannibals all ran into the audience to get a 'victim'. The place was jumping as all us kids kept yelling 'Me . . . pick me' and you may have gathered that the reason that this particular event sticks out in my mind is that I got picked.

This huge brick-coloured cannibal shook his spear at me and shouted something along the lines of: 'YOU . . . COME.'

'Is it me?' I asked looking at one of the grown-ups.

'Eh. Hurry up! On yeh go.'

Try and stop me must have been my motto as I nearly trampled my wee brother and any of the rest who were nearer the aisle than me.

I dived along the row and grabbed the cannibal by the hand, and was marched up the side steps onto the stage and into the wings of the Palace theatre.

I was going to be an actress!

Then this man instructed the wee huddled group of us to run on the stage yelling and get behind the pot. When he said 'get behind' I followed his pointing finger and had a real look at that pot: it was just the front of a pot, and it was made out of wood and painted, and there were steps up to a wee landing that we would be standing on.

I can remember feeling let down that it wasn't a real pot. Between that and Carmen Miranda's rubber ears, what next?

Anyway, I duly went on and did my turn with the rest. And we yelled and jumped and generally had a great time. I enjoyed myself to no end standing on the platform, even though I was behind the kiddie-on pot. And we each got a bag of sweeties at the end and clapped by the audience, so that was good.

But still I felt cheated about that cannibal's pot.

I remember telling my mother as we went home about it, saying that they shouldn't say it's a pot, when it's only a kiddie-on pot:

'Well did yeh no enjoy yersel?'

'Oh! Eh.'

'An wid yeh rither they wir real cannibals, an ate yeh efter they'd really bilt yeh alive?'

'No.' I would imagine that would be a definite.

'Then there yeh go. Better that it wiz kiddie-on then.'

But the feeling persisted that night about that pantomime pot (although I couldn't have explained it to anyone back then).

It was a bit like the feeling I got when the thinks-he's-smarter-than-me kid at the school let me know there was no Santa Claus. Then I ran home after school came out and questioned my mother, and she had to tell me the truth. Then she'd to explain that since there was my wee brother who was younger than me, and he still believed in Santa, I'd to stay quiet about it.

This conversation was accompanied with words like: 'You're a big lassie now, an too big tae keep believin in Santy Klazz Eh suppose.' So now I was in on the secret, but I hadn't to let on to the 'wee ane'.

And you know that while one bit of you feels grown-up, the

other bit wishes you were still the 'wee ane', and in your heart you reluctantly close the door on Santa Claus.

Well that's how I felt about that kiddie-on pot.

However . . . there was always one last, favourite thing to come came at the end of the pantomime. They would lower a huge sheet from the rafters of the theatre with the words of a pantomime song written on it. Then, one or two of the cast members would come on stage and incite one half of the hall to beat the other half at the final sing-song.

They'd take up positions at each end of the stage.

'Are you ready on my side?'

'YEEEESSSSSSSSS!'

'We can't hear you?'

'YEEEEEEEEEEEEEEEEEEEEEEEEEEESSSSSSSSSSSSSSSSSSSS'.

'By this time I would imagine the dead up at Balgay Hill could hear us.'

'Okay. Let's begin. Follow the words on the screen.'

Shades of the Saturday Cinema Club.

And off we'd go:

Santy Klazz wull no come doon yehr lum . . . **jist fir yehr cheek!**

Santy Klazz wull no come doon yehr lum . . . **jist fir yehr cheek!**

The pussy cat'll **scratch yeh!**

The boggy man'll **get yeh!**

BUHHHHHHHHTTT . . .

Santy Klazz wull no come doon yehr lum

JIST FIR YEHR CHEEK!

Great stuff indeed!

# SUNDAY VISITS AN
# THIR STORIES

When I lived in my tenement up the West End of Dundee, my paternal grandparents and my father's Auntie Mary lived up Hilltown way. And they both lived in tenements as well.

My Auntie Mary lived one stair up in her tenement. Her kitchen window faced onto an open railed platform (plettie) and her ben-the-room faced onto the street.

In those days folk who lived upstairs in a tenement some-times had the advantage of having a window that overlooked the street.

Folk would get a cushion, place it on the window sill, lean on it and survey their world at large from this vantage point, or 'hingie'. They could pass the time of day with any of their neighbours who were having a hingie of their own, or someone passing in the street below. It was not unusual for a multi-hingie to be in progress as you walked by.

But Auntie Mary disapproved of 'airin yehr business tae all an sundry oot o' the windy.' So although we were allowed a hingie (only with her present), and we could wave and say hello, and pass the time of day, we didn't see her have many conversations 'hingie-wise'. In Auntie Mary's book this 'wizna richt', and if it 'wizna richt', then it just never happened as far as she was concerned.

She was a real strong Dundee woman and a fighter most of her life, because life never gave her any other choice. Auntie Mary was in the jute mills as a part-timer when she was a child.

She was a weaver from the age of fourteen until she retired at sixty. She joined the jute workers' union when it was formed, and she took up the cudgel on behalf of anyone who 'wiz gettin taen a len o''.

She never married although there was the tale of the lad who went to fight in the 1916 war in France and never came back. She lived with, and cared for, her mother and father all their days.

She herself died at the age of ninety-four, and had lived in the same two rooms all her life. She went as far as London once, I believe. I remember her saying to me one time I was up visiting her, when she was practically house bound: 'Yeh ken Eh've lived in this hoose a meh life, an if Eh stole even one wee brick, Eh could get the bliddy jail.' And she was right!

My Auntie Mary knew more about the human condition than almost any other person I've met. She was morally good, without ever taking the moral high ground. There weren't too many shades of grey for her, but she always 'gently scanned her brother man'.

When she was young she had been a suffragette. They would meet outside the High School gates, stand on carts and attempt to get their message across to the general public. Once she told me:

'Dae yeh ken whit? Sometimes weh got booed at, an got pelted weh auld fruit an cabbages and stuff. But Eh jist picked it up an threw it richt back at them.' That was no surprise to me.

When I was about eight years old, I had stood on the Caird Hall steps with her one May Day. In my household that was quite an important day and the unions and the Labour Party used to set up a rally with floats, and folk used to go to these events with their banners.

Anyway, I was standing on the steps with Auntie Mary this particular May Day, watching as my mother clambered up onto one of the floats that represented women getting the vote. My mother was dressed as a suffragette, and I asked what this was all about.

'Thir oot there remindin ordinary fowk, especially women, that they should always yaze thir vote. So you tak a guid look, an dinna *you* ever forget that.'

I haven't.

I recall going up the outside stairs to Auntie Mary's house. These stairs were feet-hollowed in the middle. We'd knock on the 'plettie windie' and shout 'it's us' before we invaded the two tiny wee rooms. Mind you, she had an inside toilet. It was no bigger than a cubby hole, but none-the-less, it *was* an inside toilet, and there was only her.

She used to keep her mop and pail in the corner of the toilet, and all her cleaning tools on a wee shelf that had been put up on the wall. I used to play 'cleanin up the lavvie' for hours. That wee toilet shone like a bubble.

Some Sundays, weather permitting, we went on our 'jaunts tae the Hullie'. Auntie Mary's immediate family was interred in Balgay Hill Cemetery. So we would all trek over to the Hullie.

There we would take the old flowers from the graves to the bin, and bring back fresh water from the well for the new flowers. Auntie Mary carried a flask with hot water, soap, a scrubbing brush and a cleaning rag. She would tidy up the graves, and wash and polish the headstones. I think my dead relatives must have had one of the cleanest plots in the Hullie.

We never took the tramcar for our Sunday cemetery jaunts. If you complained about walking she would say: 'Good Goad, if meh auld legs kin walk tae the Hullie an back, then Eh'm shair your young legs are well able.'

My older sister tells the story of one particular Sunday when my brother must have been fed up with all this walking to and fro every week, and asked why they never got to take the tramcar.

They got the usual 'young legs' reply. Auntie Mary was at the back, they walked on in front of her, and then she overheard my brother say to my sister:

'Humph! She thinks she's savin money, but weh eat a the mair when weh get hame, an look at a' the shoe leather weh keep weystin, she's no gave much thought tae any o' that hiz she? No she hiz nutt!!'

* * *

Auntie Mary told that tale for many a year to come, but we still never got to take the tramcar if it was within what she considered walking distance.

After business was done and dusted at the cemetery, we did, however, get a Sunday treat. There was a chip shop and an ice cream shop in Hill Street. In the summer we would get a cone, and in the colder weather we got chips to eat out the bag.

Auntie Mary was our knitter-in-chief. She always had something 'on the pins' for us. She knitted enough socks in her lifetime to fit out the Black Watch. She knitted us skirts, cardigans and jumpers of all description. Oh! And loads and loads of 'dallies' clahes'. My doll must've been the envy of all who lived in doll land. Auntie Mary sewed all the curtains and took up all the hems. In fact, she did anything she could to help my family.

I was seventeen when my Auntie Mary died. It was the first time in my young adult life I'd experienced the death of someone close to my family.

My mother was absolutely bereft, and greatly missed one of her dearest friends and helpmates, for many a day to come. For the rest of her life, my mother spoke of Auntie Mary often and with great affection.

On Sundays, we would normally go over and visit 'meh ither grannie' as well. I have more memories of my grandmother than I do of my grandfather, because I was quite young when he died.

But what I do remember is that they lived one stair up in the middle of their tenement, and when I was really wee they had a huge Alsatian. This Alsatian must have been the canniest animal alive, for I can remember running around the back green holding on to his tail and him belting around like an idiot, but seldom did he snap, unless he was tired and had had enough, then one of the adults would give the poor dog a break by saying, 'Stop that (whatever it was). If that doag bites yeh it's yehr ain fault.'

My paternal grannie was a great cook and baker, and made the best rhubarb and ginger jam I have ever tasted, then or now.

My grandfather had a plot (they called it a hen run) on ground that sloped up the hill, at the back of their tenement. He called it his hen run because amongst other things he kept hens there, as well as ducks, budgies, and a cat that visited when it felt like it.

Oh! And he had a tame jackdaw, which used to perch on his bonnet as he went about the hen run.

At one time he even had a monkey there that my uncle (my father's brother) had brought home from his travels as a merchant sailor. Me and that monkey couldn't stand each other from the get go. He was nothing like Tarzan's funny and clever monkey, 'Cheetah'.

The very first time I met my uncle's monkey I got too close to the enclosed area he was running around in up at the hen run, and he reached through the mesh wire, grabbed hold of my hair, screeched like a banshee and held on.

Well if that monkey thought it could screech like a banshee then it had never heard me. My grandfather dashed out from the hen hut liked he'd been fired from a cannon, grabbed me, hit the monkey's hand until it let go then said: 'Whit the hell are yeh daen tae the monkey?'

What was *I* doing to the monkey? What was *I* doing to the monkey?

And there after began a hate-relationship between me and that monkey (he must have had a name, I just never used it). I have to admit here that the monkey did have a reason to dislike me after that, for many a sly poke he got with a stick, when no one could see me.

My grandfather used to sell some of his chickens to local folk, but there was an Indian sailor who used to come up to the hen run to buy chickens, when his boat docked in Dundee. He must have known my grandfather from somewhere, perhaps through my uncle the sailor.

The reason I remember this man was that he wanted his chicken alive when it went in the bag, as he wanted to kill it his way. Fair enough! So off he'd go, leaving with the chicken trussed up in the bag, and I can't remember it making any noise.

What I do remember about this man was he was always smiling and he always gave me a penny every time I was there, and if I missed him I was kicking myself. He did have a downside though. He liked the monkey!

I was the middle child in my family, bang in the middle of

my two brothers and two sisters. So I got the benefit of the Sunday visits twice. Firstly, with the older two and then with my younger brother. So, I had a good long run at the Sunday visits.

Each visit Auntie Mary fed us and gave us a 'Sunday penny'. Then we'd go over the road to my grandmother and get fed all over again and given more 'Sunday pennies'.

Eventually, as is the way with all generations, we grew up, and grew away from the Sunday visit routine.

We made our own friends and had things to do and places to go with them, as we began to make our own way in the world.

# STORYLAND AKA 'THE LEB'

When I was a kid my father was a voracious reader (so was my mother for that matter) and so I spent a lot of Saturday mornings, before we were let loose on the local Cinema Club, going with him to the local library, or 'The Leb' as it was known in my neck of the woods.

Usually, we'd stop just outside the close, or inside the close if it were windy, so he could light a cigarette and we could get ourselves organised, then he'd say, 'Right, are yeh ready? Well, let's go then.' Then, when we'd get so far along the road: 'So . . . whit are they readin tae yeh this week?'

I knew he knew already, for I'd recited it all coming back along the road the week before. But it let me set the stage for what was to come, and I loved that.

So I'd tell him about dragons and ships, and fairies and pirates, and dogs and cats and horses, all of whom had saved the day at one time or another. I would emphasise my part in it all with a little street theatre along the way.

I especially liked it when I was sailing with Jim Hawkins (*Treasure Island* was a great favourite of mine) and I always felt especially sad for that wee man, Ben Gunn, who, I informed my father, 'wiz nearly aff-eez-heid fir a wee buttie cheese. An ee should've lived next-door tae us, fir we wid've gave'm some'.

And that was true, for in those days it was a common practice for my mother to feed somebody else in our street. At dinner time when I came home from school there would be a bowl sitting on 'the bunker' and before I had my plate of soup she would whisk a ladle full from that never-ending soup pot and say: 'Nip tae auld Mrs/Mr so-and-so weh this, an dinna drap it!'

So I am sure she would have found some cheese for Benn Gunn.

Oh! And what about that fancy wee girl that had a horse called Black Beauty, the same first name as Dick Turpin's horse? It amazed me that a wee lassie and a highwayman should have almost the same taste in horses' names. Me, I always preferred Roy Roger's horse 'Trigger'. Now there was a *real* name that any horse would be proud of.

Storyland (for that was what the local library always was in my head) was just a stone's throw away from the tenements, the mills, a carpet factory and a coal yard.

In fact, now I come to think of it, Storyland was a sort of invisible dividing line, a border if you will, between kingdoms.

The 'Leb' straddled the border at a place called 'The Sinderins'. The houses on my side of Storyland were all bundled up together, but when you passed through the boundary at 'The Sinderins' and onto the other side, there were the posh tenements. There were some houses (some of them like hotels to me) that stood on their own, with long driveways and lots of grass. But that was past the cemetery. Some of them looked out into the cemetery, so I was very glad I didn't live there.

In fact, I always felt my side of the border was by far and away the best place to live!

So we'd reach the library.

I recall my father saying to me once when I was on a visit to the library:

'Dae yeh ken that books are the one thing that let yeh gae any place in the world, any yeh niver even leave the building? Yeh jist cross the room, an pick up a book, an aff yeh go!'

And he was dead right.

My father would push open the huge front door of the Victorian library and reading rooms.

Even before you pushed aside the velvet door curtains, you felt the velvet silence.

First of all, we would go into the big room where the walls were papered with books and real wallpaper, and up to the desk with the big rubber inkpad and stampers.

'Morning.'

'Morning.'

'Nice day (terrible day; looks like rain; looks like snow).'

He'd hand the books over. Thump-Thump. Thump-Thump. Thump-Thump.

'Thank you.' Or 'Tuppence please,' if you were handing in a late arrival.

Onto the mighty shelves (they were mighty to me back then) which protected their charges. Each had its contents named on tiny brass plaques at the end of each bookshelf.

He'd rake for books. Done.

On to my bit. I'd select my book of the week. Done.

Books taken out. Thump-Thump. Thump-Thump. Thump-Thump.

Then my father would stick the bundle of new books beneath his arm. Back out the door and into the main corridor. There we would part for a while.

He'd go to read in the huge long paper-worn tables room, selecting each newspaper in turn from its iron box on the wall.

Some Saturdays they had folk that read to the kids and I relished it. I'd depart to the scratchy carpet room, with its polished surround. It didn't take long, however, for the story-teller to iron out all the tufts on the scratchy carpet and take us on our voyage, to anyplace in the world, and ... yes ... without even leaving the room.

All too soon it seemed to me, the spinner of yarns would pick up their bookmark, thus signalling a return to the scratchy carpet room, but never, ever, without dangling before us the last sentence of the chapter of our current adventure:

'And so ... let's see what happens next time.'

And so ... we did.

# HAPPY NEW YEAR

As a kid I did, of course, love Christmas. But in my house Hogmanay was the big thing. For, sure, when you're only six or seven then of course Santa is the 'Main Man', but back then, hard on his heels, came Hogmanay.

My maternal grandparents lived next door to me. One of my aunties lived two streets away. That didn't count the friends and relatives who lived in the vicinity. And that was on my mother's side.

My father only had one brother, but on Hogmanay he would call into our house too. Then there were the 'honorary aunties and uncles'. Now here's a thing. Normally, honorary aunts and uncles usually came from my mother's pals, and that seems to be quite common as far as I can tell.

The week that led up to Hogmanay was a frenzy of cleaning. Cleaning everything.

Our public washing house along the road resembled a scene from *The Steamie*.

The rule was that if it stood still, then it got cleaned, and that included us.

On Hogmanay morning my mother would start by making a huge pot of soup, then stick another butcher's steak pie in the oven ready to be cooked (we'd already had one at Christmas).

There is nothing in this world like the crust on a butcher's bought steak pie – right into your arteries, 'an nae messin'.

Another pot of mince and big beans (haricot) got put on a peek on the stove.

Later on, when we moved to Fintry, we also got sausages and onions made in a casserole in the oven, and big flaky sausage rolls.

This was followed by the majestic Clootie Dumplin!

The Hogmanay dumpling had to be huge. So my mother used to make up the dumpling mixture, put it in a pillow case, and then boil it in the washing house boiler in the back greenie (another use for the washie). Talk about multi-functioning. Everything was multi-functioning where I lived.

It was a common practice then to tell the butcher what you would require early, and then start paying it up so that you had it all paid in time for the festivities.

My Great-Auntie Mary and my other grannie (from my father's side) made the bun and shortie, thus saving my mother the money.

So on Hogmanay, during the day, we all got farmed out to anybody who was ahead with their chores, and that let my mother get stuck in.

In Dundee when I was a kid, my father never got Christmas Day off. We used to get up and open our presents, then he'd go off to work as usual, and this was the same for most workers. But nobody I knew ever worked on Hogmanay. My own father had two days off then. He was in charge of 'the drink'.

My father wasn't much of a drinker himself, and there was never drink in the house apart from high days and holidays like New Year, and that was also the same for most folk back then. But at New Year we always had beer and whisky, and sherry or port.

We always got a bottle of raspberry cordial to toast the New

Year in. We got our drink of cordial out of the wee nip glasses with the kilties painted on the front.

The glasses would all be laid out on the kitchen table, shining like bubbles, after we had puffed all over them and cleaned them with a dish cloth. We must have been more resilient to germs in those days.

At approximately 11.15 p.m. my mother would wash the outside close and the doorstep. Then she would rinse out the last dirty dishcloth and hang it over the rail above the fireplace.

Next, she would take the brand new (but 'washed tae get the newness aff it') dish cloth, reserved especially for the occasion, which had been ironed, and put it on the hook at the side of the bunker which kept the coal, but had a sink attached to it.

The food was simmering away. The dumpling, the bun and the shortie were all laid out on the kitchen table. Jimmy Shand was on the radio.

At three minutes before midnight we all filled up our glasses. As the bells went we all hugged, shook hands and wished each other Happy New Year.

As we clinked glasses, year on year my mother repeated her usual toast of: 'Here's tae us wha's like us, dam few, an thir a deid.' To which my father would reply: 'Eh an here's hopin it's a lang time afore weh jine them.'

Then the night began.

At about one minute past midnight, somebody who'd been waiting outside would hammer on the door to be let in. Never would a red-haired person be allowed to be your first foot. Since I had copper-coloured hair then, I was never allowed to be anybody else's first foot either.

Everybody took this custom seriously. If we were first-footing someone, and I reached the door first, I automatically stepped aside and let someone else go before me, in case they hadn't had a first foot yet. But once I got inside it took a good one to beat me to the goodies.

My mother's first foot usually carried a big lump of coal. And she always got a herring done up in a frock. I have never really found out why herrings had to wear dresses, but that was another one of our 'norms' back then.

After we had been first footed and had demolished the steak pie and most of the soup we went next door to my grannie's. But mainly we stayed at home and folk came to us.

On Hogmanay in my neck of the woods it was always like how many human beings can be crammed into 'twa-rooms', and we tried our best I can tell you.

To this day I can remember the words of most of the old Irish songs. All the old Dundee street songs were trotted out each year as well, along with Nat King Cole and Sinatra and those guys.

Everybody had a party piece, with hardly any exceptions. If you protested you couldn't sing you'd be told: 'Naebody's peyin guid money tae lusten tae yeh. Thir gettin it free. So get on weh it.'

And you did! If anyone was too shy to take a turn then I'd be delighted to be volunteered, and I was in my element, for I loved a good old sing-song. I still do.

As a kid on these occasions, I would crawl under the tablecloth and sit under the kitchen table on the ledge that supported it. From that hidey-hole you could listen to all the gab, and identify each singer with their song, for they always sang the same songs that really belonged to their mother, father, brother, auntie (some of whom 'wir lang gone'), or anyone else they could think of.

I remember some woman singing about a soldier dying alone on a battlefield, and his girlfriend killing herself because he had died. This song seemed to last as long as the war had!

I remember my mother remarking the next day:

'Goad's truth, beh the time she'd feenished it wiz a guid joab we'd nae roosty razor blades.'

I asked why we needed razor blades.

'Is anybody talkin tae you, rabbit lugs?'

And that wasn't the first time that had been said.

If you can't imagine folk trying to do an eightsome reel in an eight foot by ten foot room, then believe me it was absolutely possible. Sometimes folk would pile the table and chairs up on the bed in the bed recess.

The gramophone ('grammie' and there we go again with the '-ie' thing) would be cranked up. Jimmy Shand would be put up as loud as possible. No caring about 'the neeghbours next door or up-the-stairs' on this night, for they were making their own noise. Then off they'd go, hoochin and skirlin.

Sometime in the early hours, us kids were all carted ben-the-room or back home and dropped into bed. Nine times out of ten somebody else's kids would land there along with us, and for us, another Hogmanay had bitten the dust.

But there was one more treat.

On New Year's Day our breakfast was always black pudding, bacon, eggs and fried dumpling. Food for the Gods right enough!

As an adult, every Hogmanay, the last things I do, even if I am not going to be in my own house, are shake out the door mat, sweep the landing, wash out the dirty dish cloth and hang it up to dry.

Then I put out the new rinsed and ironed dish cloth on a hook in the kitchen and give my mother a smile.

I wouldn't feel right about the approaching New Year if I didn't, and as I hang up my new dishcloth, I think of my mother and back then.

# THE CO-OPIE

As well as the wee specialist shops that served our community, one of the streets along from where I lived housed a co-operative (the co-opie aka 'the Sosh').

In Dundee, there was the Scottish Co-operative Wholesale Society (SCWS) and the Dundee Eastern Co-operative Society (DECS), but I can't recall which one was in my neighbourhood, as it was always referred to as 'the Sosh' by anyone I knew!

This was our equivalent of a supermarket. You couldn't pay by credit card, for we had none, but you could get credit for the week, which was called 'tick', and then you cleared it off.

Folk who let their 'tick' pile up so that they couldn't clear their debt got spoken about, so running up debt on your 'Soshie Book' was something to keep quiet about, and not a desired thing to do.

And in my house it was tantamount to a disgrace not to 'pey yehr wey' according to my father. And he was like that to the end of his days. Wonder what he'd think now?

So, like most folk who used the co-opie, we shopped for some things there all week, and then cleared the book on Friday.

When you shopped there you were given a numbered

receipt (that was your own unique number) with the amount of money you had spent on it, and they were called checks. Twice a year your money was tallied and you were then paid out a dividend ('divi' to us). Although I think the other shops had 'a book' for their trusted customers, the 'Sosh Book' was the official one for food shopping, and the only one that I know of that paid out dividends.

This shop had wooden floorboards and wooden counters. You would go in and place your book through the slat in a wooden box which sat on the counter. It was a fair system of first come, first served, and saved many a rammy. The books would pile up in order; the assistant would take a book from the bottom of the pile and shout out your name.

I loved the counter that had the huge tub of butter on a board. When you ordered butter the assistant would place a piece of greaseproof paper on the board, hook out a lump of butter, get the butter skelpers, and wallop away until it was a nice square shape. I was fascinated by the speed with which this was achieved.

The same counter had a cheese board, and the assistant would cut off a lump of cheese with the wire, and they were whizzes at getting just the right quantity.

Biscuits were sold loose. They had boxes that were set lengthwise in a long wooden case, and the lids of the boxes were made of glass so that you could see the biscuits.

Tea was taken from boxes sat on the back of the counters, and shovelled into brown paper bags. So were porridge oats and many other goods.

My very first job when I left school was working in the Check Office of the SCWS at the bottom of the old Wellgate. Part of my job was to count the checks and put them into the slots on the boards that were provided.

The boards had dozens of slots, and as a check was two

inches by one inch, and there were loads of them, then you could imagine that some days I was about bored to death with the whole thing, so I knew that wasn't going to last long.

But I did like the twice-yearly pay-out days, when folk came for their 'divi'. Sometimes the queue would be really long, and folk would wait in line, and then wander round the store seeing what they could buy.

Now you can sit in your house, switch on a computer, and off you go into the whole world as your supermarket and shopping centre.

Talk about time changing things at a speed of knots.

# MARSHALL'S, A BUSTER, THEN A SASS

Saturday was book shop, buster and Sass day.

Early Saturday evening we would all get cleaned up and walk from my tenement at the West End down past the Coffin Mill, and on to Marshall's bookshop at the bottom of the Scourin Burn.

I loved that bookshop.

It was floor to ceiling with books. You could've gone in the door at one year old and got buried in there, and I bet you still wouldn't have read all those books.

It was the 1940's version of a swap shop.

You bought your first comic for tuppence. If you didn't destroy it then you could exchange it for another comic the next Saturday, and you were only charged a penny for the new comic.

I remember one comic that got destroyed because I was fighting with my older brother about who should get first read of what.

We always kept the noise down in case we were heard. Even if we did land up ben-the-room and it turned into a shoving match, then it had to be a Charlie Chaplin fight, so named by my brother because you couldn't shout at each other in case my father heard you. And thumping each other was absolutely 'Verboten'! We must have gotten carried away and the 'It's Mine! No, it's no, it's MINE!' must have gotten louder to the point that it could be heard in the room next door.

The door opened. My father walked across the room, tore the comic in half across the way, handed me the top half, my brother the bottom half – 'There yeh go. Now yeh've baith got a comic.' – closed the door and went back to whatever he was doing.

My brother glowered at me and muttered: 'Well, Eh kin tell yeh this much, it's your comic that's got toarn, an yeh'll no get money back fae Marshall's now.'

I bet that started another silent movie fight!

Anyway, we used to get two comics apiece each week, read them, swap them with each other, then take them back and swap them for two more new ones. But, as I've said, Mr. Marshall only took back comics that weren't damaged, so you had to be careful when you were reading them.

I think that's where I first got my love of adventure stories, and soon developed a taste for this kind of tale. To this day, give me a good old murder or horror story.

My mother would get her detective magazines, which she also got half price as long as she handed the old ones back, and my father got his books. I can't remember him ever picking just one type of book; I think he read just about every-thing that he could lay hands on.

So after the dealings with Marshalls's bookshop were over, the books and comics were packed away in the Marshall's bookshop message bag, hung on the back of the Tansad and we headed for the busters.

All these trips had starts and stops as we met other folk we knew who were 'oot fir a Seterday dander'. Then my parents would have to 'pass the time o' day weh them'.

Once the busters were in sight I used to hope that we wouldn't meet anybody else, because then it was a form of torture to me, to be so near the feeding grounds and yet have to listen to more talk before I could 'get stuck in'.

At last!!

The buster stalls were two big canvas tents, with wooden walls, I think. They were just down from Birrell's shoe shop in the Overgate. The buster stalls were the equivalent of today's MacDonald's. And the busters were always 'hoachin' on a Saturday.

The inside of the tent had wooden benches all round its walls. There was a huge brazier in the middle of the room, and the coals were always white hot (the Health and Safety would have had a fit). There were huge black frying pots and huge pots of buster peas. The cost of the portions in old money started at tuppence, then fourpence, and sixpence. The plates were accordingly, a wee pudding plate, a medium pudding plate, and a soup plate.

We always got a tuppenny plate, and if we finished that (you should have seen the speed, and the awful death, that first buster got), then we usually got another tuppence for a second plate.

One of the ladies who ran the busters used to call out to folk: 'Come in, come in, fat peas and lang chips.' And they were!

Sometimes, if I was with my grannie, she would bring bread and butter, and we dipped up the pea juice that was mixed with a huge lashing of salt and vinegar.

But my mother used to wrinkle her nose at this, so on Saturday it was always a breadless buster, which went down without touching the sides as usual.

I think it was the early 1950s when the buster stalls shut down, but I have many happy memories of enjoying a buster, and you know what? You can get all the ingredients (ham bones, marrowfat peas and potatoes), but I have never been able to make, or get, a buster quite like the old Overgate ones. Maybe it was the open air that made them taste so good (that sounded like one of the statements that would have also been made about the mince in *The Steamie*).

Dietitians would have had a fit at our diet back then, and I know it couldn't have been doing my arteries any good, but to this day (when I do eat much more healthily), I have never tasted a lettuce leaf that even comes within a moon's distance of my mother's 'tatties, mince an big beans, weh doughballs'. And that goes for a buster as well!

Buster over, we'd meet someone else, and my mother would 'pass some mair time o' day'.

Then, last but not least, we'd cross over from the busters and into Greenhill's Sarsaparilla Shop and meet up with my father, who never came with us to get a buster.

I just got to thinking, and I've never asked anyone, but I think Greenhill's must have been a chemist as well, but I can only remember everybody coming in there 'fir a Sass'.

The Sass shop had a long polished wooden counter, with a rail which ran along the bottom of the floor, just like an old pub. The walls had all the polished wee boxes in them. The jars of powder for the drinks always fascinated me.

Mr. Greenhill, the Sass man, had a spoon with a long handle made especially for the job. He used to dip into the jar after you'd make your choice, put it into either a small, medium or large glass, and then fill it up with water. Then he'd stir it all up vigorously and it would go all fizzy. There was orange, lemon, raspberry, strawberry and another flavour, which I can't remember, and then there was the original sass. I always chose raspberry or lemon.

The original sass was black in colour and tasted of liquorice.

My father used to down a huge glassful in the same time that we had one wee glass, but he always left some of his drink so we all had a wee drop of that too, if we wanted.

I was never much taken up with the original sass, but a 'Coloured Sass' was definitely just the job for washing down your buster.

Then we'd start off on the trek homeward, up the Overgate again, up the West Port, past the pawn shop, and a pub called 'The Rattie' (Rat Hole). I used to think as a kid, 'Imagine crehin yehr pub the same name as a rat. Naebody likes rats.'

But I'm sure somewhere in the annals of Dundee history there's an answer.

And finally, back along the Hawkhill ('Hackie' to the residents) to the 'Warkie Roadie'.

Going home we'd meet somebody else, and my parents would 'pass the time o' day weh them' as well.

I think half the time was taken up blethering, but it gave us time to run around with the rest of the kids and create orderly mayhem (remember they-who-must-be-obeyed were present).

Little did I think then that in the years to come I'd be walking the same streets in the 'Monkey's Parade', and I'd be the one doing all the blethering, but by then it was a new type of blether called 'chatting up'.

# LOTIONS AN POTIONS AN WHISPERIN

I think there's a Viking alive and well inside me, because I prefer the cold to the heat. My windows are open summer and winter, and I absolutely love when the rain is battering down and the wind is blowing up a storm. Mind you, that's when I'm in my living room, not on a long boat!

When I was wee I can remember my mother dragging me back in the house to tie up my pixie (which usually trailed down the back of my neck practically choking me), and force on these mitts that were tied together with elastic and shoved up the arms of my coat, so that I wouldn't lose them, thus the elastic knocked socks off the back of my neck, whilst the pixie attempted to strangle me.

Oh! Yeh! And what about the scarf (usually one of your father's) that was wrapped round your chest and pinned at the back with the hugest safety that your mother could lay her hands on? At least you'd be warm when you fell backwards and impaled yourself on the pin.

The other thing I hated with a vengeance was my liberty bodice. That was stuck under my jumper in the winter because I 'wiz runnin aboot like a forkie, an wid NUT shut meh coat'.

My mother never worked out the logic that I was *sweating* to death.

And that liberty bodice had tapes tied on the front and the back to hold up your woollen stockings that you wore in winter time.

If my mother was in a hurry when she was putting on my stockings she'd say: 'Stand up strecht or yehr stockins'll be a wrang.'

If I didn't listen to her as she tied up my stockings, 'a wrang' meant that I walked about bent over like Quasi Modo all day.

My solution to that was to pick holes in my stockings and say I'd fallen. The holes also let the air in and that suited me fine. It was getting my mother to believe that I fell that was usually the problem.

And do you remember that camphorated oil? If I had a cold, that oil got heated up on a spoon and then rubbed all over my chest and back, and if you couldn't breathe a good old rub of it went under your nose as well.

Good job my pyjamas weren't nylon, or I would've been slipping out the bed. But I never caught a lot of anything when I was young, if memory serves me.

So as a kid, when all around me were huddling up, I used to wait until I got around the corner and open my coat, pull off my pixie, leave the mitts hanging and take off.

The kids nowadays have my envy. I would have loved all the lightweight padded coats when I was a kid. I love them now. It's great that you can wear a tee-shirt, and just don one of these thermal coats. In the winter when I was a kid, I went to bed with more on than I go outside in now.

Then there was the cure for toothache. My mother would fill a sock with hot salt and stick it under your chin, or as much as possible on the sore area, and say: 'There yeh go. It'll be gone afore yeh kin say Jeck Roabson.'

Yet another example of how my mother used Jeck Roabson to fit almost any occasion.

But a big dread was if you caught NITS in your hair.

I never realised as a kid that anybody could get nits, and the thought of catching them in my hair must've horrified me so much that I have no recollection of having them at all, but when I speak to folk in my age group it was quite common.

What I really dreaded, truth be known, was that the brown lady (nurse) that visited the school would find any, because then you were put behind the blackboard with the rest of the Nit folk, so that she could talk to you in private.

Private I ask you. Even a kid of six or seven knew that if you had to stand behind the blackboard after she looked through your hair then . . . YOU HAD THE NITS!

So it was with this in mind that I suffered the torments of the bone comb in silence (well maybe that's an exaggeration), but I suffered.

My mother would wash my hair, then lay out a newspaper on the floor, pour some stuff over my hair that stank like an open cesspit to me, and begin to drag the bone comb through it. That was one of the times it would have been a godsend to have had thin hair.

If I complained too much at this pulling and tugging, whilst I kept an alert eye on the newspaper for any sign of 'them', then I'd be told: 'Dae yeh want me tae find them if thir there, or the brown lady?' No contest!

We were once shown picture slides at the school which showed the nits louping the length of the playground from one head to another, and we were told to never wear someone else's pixie, or any form of headwear from someone else.

Well I didn't have to be told twice. I guarded my hat like it was the crown jewels right enough.

And another thing you could get was impetigo, but I think you were a lot less likely to get that than 'the nits'. I think I would have really had a fit if I'd ever got impetigo.

For some poor wee souls practically got their hair shaved off if they got it in their heads. So how could you hide that? And even worse, they treated it with purple-coloured stuff that made you definitely stand out in the crowd.

Once I went beneath the table in my grandmother's house, dragging my wee brother with me. I had decided I would play barbers. So I cut his hair with the scissors that I'd nicked from the drawer. Then I chopped off my ponytail and fringe. Then the poor cat decided to come under the table, got jumped on, and despite putting up a good fight, got sat on and his whiskers clipped. And that was when I was found out.

My grandmother had the vapours when she saw her cat staggering because it had now lost its balance (a cat's whiskers, I was to learn, give it the spacial awareness it requires).

I got spacial awareness right enough as I got thumped for what I'd done to my brother and the cat, and was frog-marched down to the barber with my brother, and we both got an impetigo haircut. My mother was fuming:

'Look at the twa o' yeh? Yehr like war orphins. Eh'm no carin aboot you, but look it whit yehv'e done tae yehr wee brither. Yehr lucky yehr stull in one buht.'

Common sense told me not to say what worried me the most was that folk might think I had nits, so I just held my tongue.

Now, one of the things that I remember puzzled me for

years was the way my mother and her friends spoke about anything that had to do with 'women's stuff or death'.

The conversation might start off on a normal note but when it got to the bits they did not want broadcast by little ears and big mouths, then it went into a mime that would have passed muster on any stage.

Of course, the minute the voices went to a whisper, your ears cocked up:

'Did yeh hear aboot auld Mrs/Mr Whatever-the-name-was? Thiv got . . .' (fade to a whisper).

'Yehr jokin? Whit a shame, puir auld sowel. But mind yeh somebody wiz tellin me . . .' (fade to a whisper).

'Wull hiv tae get somethin an hand it in . . .' (fade to a whisper).

And so on.

If you let on you were listening, then you got shoved out the room. If they really didn't want you to hear, then you got put out anyway.

And sometimes even now, when I see a fancy bowl of fruit all done up in its cellophane, I reflect on the fact that, when I was a kid, anybody who got a bowl of fancy fruit handed in was 'no weel' right enough.

Then there was the 'Broon Paper cure'. For a chest cold you'd soak the paper in vinegar and stick it on your chest. I can't remember this happening to me. In fact, I don't remember being ill for any length of time at all. But I do remember smelling some kid that had the 'vinegar broon paper' on.

I don't remember this myself, but my mother told me that the doctor used to cost two and sixpence before the National Health came into being, so lots of times you just tried to cure the thing yourselves, or get something from the chemist.

But she always said what a good and kind man we had for our doctor. She said folk must've owed him a fortune in two and sixpences by the time the National Health was created.

As always, when I recall these childhood things, I am more than thankful that my own family stayed healthy, for there were lots of ailments eliminated that were pretty awful to catch when I was wee.

But more than that I am grateful that health-wise those days are gone forever.

# PLENTY TAE DAE AN A
# POT O' IRISH STEW

My young world was of the streets that surrounded me. The shops were round the corner. The relatives were round about. The school was five minutes one way. The cinemas were five minutes the other way. The library was about a seven-minute walk away. The churches and chapels were within a stone's throw. The Labour Party Halls and the Railwaymen's Halls were another stone's throw.

There were four jute mills, two public wash/bath houses (washies), and various other shops, chippers, ice creamers, and wee cafés.

We had a game we played after we had come charging out of the Saturday Cinema Club. Do you know if a mob of kids went careering along the streets at the same time nowadays somebody would call the police, for we must have looked like Mulligan's Army? But folk back then just thought, 'Och that's the Seterday Club oot.'

Well, the mills in these days all had big bells at the door to the porter's lodge, right at the front of the building. So we'd dive in and ring them as we flew past. If they'd been rung a few times before by some of the other Saturday Club desperados, and the porter was just behind the door waiting for you, then you got a bigger fright than you would've got from Dracula, but that was the risk we enjoyed.

Then you'd go into the shop that sold the biscuits, and ask if they had any broken biscuits (broken biscuits were sold in bags and were cheaper). When the person behind the counter replied that they did, then you said, 'Well, mend them then,' and immediately dived for the door.

Another brave thing to do, as far as we were concerned, was to jump on the back of the Scaffies' Wagon.

The bins were emptied into one big container attached to the back of the cabin, and the container had a ledge on the back that the bin men jumped on and off. When they were finished for the day, they would all pile into the front of the vehicle to go back to the depot.

My older brother always saw an empty back step on the scaffies' wagon as a personal challenge, and one Saturday as it passed us he grabbed my hand and said, 'Jump.'

And jump we did, then it speeded off and whizzed along the street, and we couldn't get back off again. I remember my hair flying straight out, and I had my brother in a right old strangle hold.

Thankfully, an adult, who spotted our predicament, frantically signalled the man who was driving the wagon. The driver ground to a halt and jumped out threatening in no uncertain terms what was going to happen to us when his boot found our posterior. But we were long gone.

However, we had been spotted and reported on by some spy, and when we arrived home to she-who-must-be-obeyed, I began to think I'd have been better off with the scaffie!

You've heard of self-contained houses? Well we were self-contained communities.

My father used to say if the man next door sneezed, we all caught cold.

My older brother used to say to me that if the man next door had beans for his tea we all farted.

I attended the Martyrs' Church Brownies where I was in the elves (I leave it to your imagination as to what comments that drew from my parents, almost as much as when I was in the fairies). I played the triangle in the Salvation Army Band of Hope for youngsters, and we got a drink and a bit of dumpling at the end of that.

I went to any kind of social evening at the church up the road. I went with my grannie to the Catholic Mothers' Group. I went on the Communist Party Picnics with my father, the Railwaymen's Children's Socials with one of my dad's pals, and the Labour Party picnics with just about everybody else I knew.

In fact I went any place where I could get a good dive about and a laugh.

And we had plenty of places to go and plenty of things to do, and in a safe area, for we were known to almost everybody where I lived.

In the run up to election time we went down to the Labour Party Hall where they were making banners and getting ready for what float they would be putting into the May Day Parade. There was a wee song that I'm sure some of you will remember all the words of, but it went something like this:

Vote! Vote! Vote! For . . . (whoever your man was)
Heez the man tae gie yeh ham an eggs.
If yeh dinna vote fir, then we'll pit yehr windies in,
An ye'll niver get tae hae a vote aghen.

Well, we ran around singing this until I bet some folk felt like 'pittin oor lights oot'.

When I think about it, a song about breaking someone's

window could hardly be put forward as a reasonable argument. But that was then.

As there was no television, along with reading, listening to the radio was a favourite pastime.

My father fitted up speakers in the kitchen and through to the room, so we could listen to the radio when we were in bed. He could cut off the sound in the kitchen, or the bedroom, so that he and my Mother would get some peace, or he could leave it on, depending what the programme was, and we could all listen.

My mother was always into murder/mystery stories. One of her favourite radio programmes was *The Man in Black* read by one Valentine Dyall. If we stayed real quiet and they forgot to turn our speakers off, we got to listen to him too.

That programme was responsible for many of my childhood nightmares. My sister would lie in bed with her fingers stuck in her ears whispering: 'Is it a ower yet?' To which my elder brother would hiss from his 'shakie-doon' on the floor: 'Shhhhh! They'll hear yeh, an then they'll turn oor speakers aff.'

My younger brother, who slept in a chair that folded down into a bed, never uttered a word. He was either sleeping or petrified. Anyway, he was too wee to understand. But I loved it! There was something very satisfying in stealing a listen to good old Valentine.

I loved fancy-dress 'dos' as well. On one occasion the brownies were having a fancy dress party. I had forgotten to tell my Mother, and only remembered on the day of 'the Brownies' pehrty'. I came tearing in from school and informed my mother that I had to have a fancy dress by teatime, or I'd be the only one there who'd just be in my Brownie uniform.

My Mother, saviour of all, said to me, 'Let me hae a think.'

And think she did, and then conjured up a small miracle! I went as 'A POT OF IRISH STEW'.

My Mother threw one of my old frocks on me. Then she sewed a carrot, a bit turnip, a leek, a potato and an onion onto an old belt, and tied the adorned belt round my waist. She tore a picture of a cow out of one of our old books and stitched it onto the back of my frock, with a wee note pinned beneath it saying: 'I'm a pot of Irish Stew.' Then . . . she gave me a POT to stick on my head!

I can just imagine today's reaction to that last statement. But it was only a wee aluminium pannie, and I think she made sure it wouldn't slip first.

Then again, that would've given her some peace for a wee while, so you never know.

Oh! And I got *second* prize at the fancy dress 'do'.

My mother lived into old age, and one of her favourite sayings was: 'Yaze whit yeh hiv, an yeh'll niver wahnt.'

Too true Ma!

# THE SATURDAY
# CINEMA CLUB

One of the absolute joys of my childhood, which I cherish within me to this day, were my trips to the Saturday Cinema Club, which was held in the local cinema called 'The Princess'.

The Princess Cinema had a very posh front which was imported from some place in far-off England, and had a fancy old-time theatre façade, and steps with rails that led you into the cinema. Then you entered the building and discovered that the walls were made of brick and corrugated iron and there was linoleum on the floors. This building featured large in the land of my childhood, my imagination and my daydreams. Some years ago I bought a painting of 'The Princess'. It hangs in my living room. That way I can enjoy a visit back there any time I want.

My Mother said the Saturday Club was worth every penny it cost her. She called it the 'Sanity Club'. She would take us along late morning, where we would join the queue to get in. Once we were up at the foyer, she would take off with the Tansad, and just enjoy only having 'the bairn' to look after for a short while.

The Saturday Club had the dear seats, that cost ninepence, and the cheap seats, that cost sixpence.

My Mother always gave us ninepence, because the sixpenny seats 'ruined yehr eyes'.

She told us if we went to the sixpenny seats, she would know by the shape of our eyes when she met us as we came out after the show.

This worked for a while, until one Saturday morning when my big hero in Kiddie-on-Land, who doubled as my older brother in real life said:

'Eh dinna think the shape o' yehr een cheenges jist cause o' the seat yehr sittin in at the pictures. Weh'll spend thruppence, and go tae the sixpenny seats. Then see whit happens when we meet Ma efter on. Mind now, nut a word!'

Seemed like a good idea to me, until after the show came out and we were running up the side road of the cinema, then I began to 'hiv meh doubts'.

The very first thing my Mother said when she spied my brother was: 'Whit on earth's wrang weh yehr eyes?' We froze in our tracks. She continued: 'Yeh look like a frog? It's like yehr tryin tae pop yehr een oot o' thir sockets. Stop that right now!' He did!

The only thing she'd noticed was him trying to be 'normal'. We never let on to her about our dodge. It gave us an extra thruppence each Saturday. Little did we know that us thinking we were one step ahead suited her just dandy. It stopped us asking for any extra money.

My mother was a natural psychologist, and never even knew it.

Each Saturday morning they had sing-alongs before the show. The words came up on the screen, and the word you were meant to be singing was highlighted by a small bouncing ball. But since everyone pleased themselves what they sang, what words they sang and at what tempo, it was just one big free-for-all. Considering the whole idea was to yell and shout anyway, we were all happy as linties.

The pictures were the least of the excitement. Sure there were Roy Rogers and Trigger, Zorro, Laurel and Hardy, Abbot and Costello, Pearl White . . . I could go on and on, for there were many. Arguing who was our favourite, and better than any of the rest, was sure to start a good old rammy.

But it was the hidden entertainment provided by the Cinema Club that I loved the most. After the sing-along, we had the Club Promise with 'The Chief', who happened to double as the manager of the cinema. She/He called upon the patrons of the Saturday Club to say the 'Promise'. This was a pledge to encourage children to act responsibly. You had to promise to obey your parents, the teacher, the boabies, your grandparents and, of course, your King!

Well . . . we promised to be good for evermore, to love and obey all and sundry, and did so with great gusto and feigned sincerity. We knew the morning's entertainment wouldn't start otherwise.

First, we had the usual racket of the sing-along-to-the-bouncing-ball session.

Then *at last*, the lights went down, and all bets were off.

We jumped on each other with boundless enthusiasm. My brother could vault these seats one handed, better than Black Beard the Pirate could leap over the yardarm.

We would spit orange-peel bullets through the air at our enemies with great relish. We attained this ammunition by buying two rotten oranges from the fruiterer, but the contents of the orange were irrelevant, it was the skin we were after.

We wrestled over the rows in front, and behind. We helped the cowboys beat the Indians, or the Indians beat the cowboys, depending whose side you were on that week

We dodged the ushers' torches when they attempted to

spotlight the culprits. But we were too many for them, and far too well trained in Cinema-Club combat.

We dodged these ushers like Zorro dodged the wicked Mexican Generals, but I bet Zorro didn't have half as much fun as us. If you did get caught and you'd been warned more than once, you were forcibly ejected by one of the torch-brandishing Evil-Usher-Banditos, and expelled to sit on the cinema steps outside. There to wait for your mother, or whoever was collecting you, to take you home.

Woe betide us if my mother came early to pick us up, and we didn't have time to hide in with the crowd who came hurtling up the lane at the end of the cinema session. She'd stand two feet away, hand on hip:

'Whit a showin up in front o' abody. Letting the hale neebourhood ken yeh'd been threw oot o' the pictures cause yeh couldna behave yersels fir fehve meenits.'

This was usually accompanied by getting grabbed by the shoulder and shaken like a rabbit, or whacked across the back of the shoulder, or shoved sideways. Thankfully, the crime had to be akin to murder before you were treated to all three at once.

The Saturday Club always finished with some heroine, usually Pearl White, tied to the railway lines as the Puffing Billy thundered towards her. Or she was hanging out of a train window clutching onto a thread, as the train hung over the deepest ravine in the world. Good old Pearl just hung there, waiting for next Saturday's episode to begin. She survived anything the baddies threw at her.

But that never surprised us. We knew she would. She lived in our cinema, in our neck of the woods!

As Pearl got tied to the line, or hung out the train, and the music went 'Dan-de-ran-dan-daaaaaaaaaaan', I'd wrap my cardigan, or coat, round my waist, tie my pixie, or hankie, round my mouth el-bandito style, then gird my loins to mosey on up the lane to meet my Ranchero-in-Chief.

The wee Head Usher with the doo-catcher's hat that was meant for somebody else's heid, took his life in his hands every week as we all rushed towards the exits, with him brandishing his torch, which we expertly dodged, and him screaming at the top of his voice: 'Hold it! Hold it! Are yeh a deaf? Get back a buht . . . back a buht Eh sade! Stop runnin up they aisles.'

Then with a mighty crash he'd fling open the fire exit doors and whip back against the wall like Spider Man. I bet that wee man took up lion taming when he got fed up of being an usher at our Saturday Club.

Finally, just like in a John Wayne film, we would ride up the lane, one for all and all for one, whipping our thighs, urging our horses to a faster gallop, celebrating another wonderful Saturday morning adventure. We would yell the last song of the day at the top of our voices, as we rode off into the sunset:

We are the Musky Riders.
The tuppenny sliders.
The penny co-ho-ho-hooooooooooooooooooones!

* * *

Then, there she was, as ever, one hand on the Tansad, the other clutching the small separate brown paper bags with an iced cake or a Paris bun in them, waving the bags to us from the top of the lane, where she stood waiting to lead us back to the old homestead.

Yippee Aye Oh! Kyaaeeeeeee!!

# PRIESTS AN NUNS

As an adult I confess to not having a particular formal belief or religion.

I was brought up with a background that consisted of Catholic, Scottish Protestant, Communist, believe-anything-yeh-like, and a suffragette thrown in for good measure.

In my house it was known for friends of my father to come and sleep on my floor before a march the next day. And what some people would call a 'rammy' was just a good old debate in my house.

My maternal grandmother, who lived next door to me, was Catholic, and it was in her house that I first got introduced to priests and nuns.

When I was a child the parish priests and nuns used to come and visit my grannie on a regular basis, and since she lived next door to me I became acquainted with them. The nuns I met in those days dressed in long grey dresses with white overalls on top, and white-winged hats.

I became fascinated with one old Irish nun in particular (well she was old to me back then). I was absolutely entranced with her big white-winged hat. I would always seek her out if she was visiting my grandmother, just to gaze at her hat. It reminded me of the wings on my angel scraps that I was collecting.

When she came to visit my grannie I would borrow her gloves, her umbrella and her 'wee' rosaries. She wore her great big rosary round her waist that nearly touched the floor.

When they were sitting having a blether, I would parade about ben-the-room pretending I too was a nun. My grannie's cat must have been the best blessed cat in our street, although getting him to sit still whilst I did the blessing was another matter altogether.

I always got the feeling that cat never had too much time for me!

I knew that being a nun could be a good thing, because when I asked my grannie what nuns did, she told me that they helped people and looked after them, and that they went away to Africa to look after the children there. In fact (according to my grannie) they went all over the world.

One day, I asked if I could borrow her (the nun's) 'hat'. My grandmother had a quick intake of breath, but the nun merely said that 'no, she did not take her hat off'.

I enquired if that was never, not even in the bath, or in bed, and she said yes, she did take it off in the bath and when she went to bed.

After the days the nun had visited, I think I must have gone on about this woman in my home, much to my father's consternation. And because I knew he wasn't happy about it, I immediately shut up. What I didn't realise at the time, and what my mother was to inform me of years later, was that he was concerned I would think that becoming the real thing would be a good idea. Apparently her reply to this was: 'Eh'd feel mair sorry fir them, if that ever happened.'

But it was the parish priest who came to call that I held in awe, because my grannie treated him special.

On the priest's allotted visiting days, and if I was around, my grannie would give me instructions that if I saw him 'goin intae ane o' the closes roond aboot', then I was to run in and let her know he was 'in the neeghbourhood'.

So, whenever I did spot him, I duly ran in and reported like the place was burning down that, 'EEZ HERE!'

Well then, you never saw such a stramash! She whipped into frenzy. Papers that were lying about were stuck below chairs. Dishes that were in the sink got a lick and a promise and crashed away, the biscuits that usually got eaten from their paper bag were put on a plate. Last, and this was the one that fascinated me, the wireless or the gramophone got *turned off*.

Do you know when I was wee I used to think that priests didn't like music, for any time they (or nuns or doctors for that matter) appeared, the wireless usually got banished to silence.

Anyway, there we were, ready and waiting. I say 'we' for I was never one to miss an opportunity to meet a person who could cause a stir. So I'd sit there with my grannie, her with her 'peeny wheeched aff', waiting patiently for 'him' to appear. The knock duly came.

'Oh! It's you father? This is a surprise!' were her first words as she opened the door.

When I enquired once why she spoke that way, and she'd known from the minute he'd appeared in the street he was coming, she would tell me to, 'Mind yehr ain business.'

We say that to kids regularly, don't we? Just to shut them up, when we're either pretending we like being in a particular situation and we don't, or we have no explanation but we want to justify it. But I was yet to be schooled in all that social palavering.

So then, the priest would sit down and usually accepted the cup of tea that was offered (that man must've been floating in tea by the number of houses he visited in my neighbourhood).

I behaved myself all through him being told who I was (again). Then related that I was, of course, doing all that I was told and behaving at school, obeying my parents and, in general, being a wee saint (pardon the pun).

I recall asking my mother when I was older, why adults were perpetually asking kids if they are behaving themselves. And it still goes on to this day. Her reply: 'It's because yeh wahnt abody tae think yehr bairns are perfect, jist like *you* do! But how kin they be perfect, when *you're* no?'

I bet some psychologists would have taken at least three chapters to say that!

Anyway back to the priest sitting in my grannie's kitchen.

I went through all the rigmarole of sitting and waiting for him, simply because there was always a 'goodie' at the end of it. And, after I got the desired biscuit or whatever, I'd whip it quick out the door before they got to the serious speaking or prayer bit. Fooling him and I don't think!

This particular day as I passed him, he said, 'You're a right well behaved wee girl, put out your hand.' And into my hand he placed a shiny new penny. You'd think he'd given me a King's ransom.

He never knew how easy it was to behave when he was there. For any monkey business and I'd have been exiled for all time when he visited, and then I wouldn't have got an extra goodie because he had called.

But I have to say the penny was a bonus.

And I also used to wonder if the priest and the nun who called in next door to me ever found out about peoples' misdemeanours, since behaving was always top of the list.

Well if they did, they never heard it from me. I wasn't about to chuck a regular supply of biscuits!

# SECRETS AN BIG HOLY HAT

On occasion, if I felt like it, I could attend the chapel on Sunday with my grandmother. If she was going there we kids could go with her as long as we stayed quiet during the mass.

I can remember her telling me once about taking my older brother to mass for the first time, and if you'd known him, then you would know that him keeping quiet or still for more than five minutes should have been a declared miracle right enough. Then my grannie said he leaned over and said to her:

'Eh need tae go tae the lavvie!'

'No yeh dinna!'

'Eh! Honest injun! Eh do!'

'Wheest!'

'Eh need tae GO!' said in a loud whisper that got more 'wheests' from the assembly.

'Fir Goad's sake the lavvie's in the church hall next door!' (The next stage is he gets poked. Yes, God did allow poking if you weren't behaving.)

'But Grannie, Eh'll jist yaze the same ain as a them!' says my brother pointing to the confessional booths.

It was on one of these Sunday outings that I first fell in love with the old Irish nun, and more importantly, her big white-winged hat.

Sometimes, when this nun was visiting my grandmother and I was there she would mysteriously pin holy medals onto my vest. When she did this, my grandmother would just wink and say, 'That's oor wee secret.'

But when I announced I had another hidden holy medal, my mother would glare at me, then whisk it off before my father could say a word, but I knew that look! If I asked what the problem was I was informed that it 'wiz nain o' meh business', or another mysterious saying of my mother's like 'mind yehr ain mindins'. They both meant, of course, 'Shut Up!'

Anyway this never seemed a big deal to me.

That is, until one day when I was eavesdropping.

Eavesdropping is a bad idea, even when it is unintentional. I think I was seven or eight years old when I uncovered what a bad idea listening in to other folks' conversation was.

I was playing outside on the pavement beneath my grandmother's kitchen window when 'Big Holy Hat' appeared. 'Big Holy Hat' was my older brother's secret name for my nun. And that's another thing. I believed, because he told me: 'She hings upside doon fae the rafters o' the chapel at night, an they hats are tae cover ehr pointed ears.'

On enquiring of my mother the validity of this statement she shook her head and merely said: 'Eh think that laddies brehns wid be better in eez pocket fir thir wasted in eez heid! Whit dae yeh lusten tae him fir?'

On getting no answer at all I decided that I didn't care what she did or where she hung up when she went to bed. I liked her.

So . . . Eavesdropping Day began like it was just a day. 'Big Holy Hat' appeared down the street. She smiled as usual, touched the top of my head, and went indoors.

After the hellos, the ensuing conversation was floating out the window and over my head until these words issued from my grandmothers mouth: 'Och. Eez a guid enough man tae them a! It's jist a' this communist rubbish. Eh jist worry about thae bairns' souls.'

My ears cocked up. Did I have a soul? And if I did what was the worry about it? The priest certainly said we all had one.

My father on having this repeated to him would start on about organised religion, whatever that was I had no clue, and even less interest as to what souls were all about.

And what had that to do with my father? Anyway, if he was involved there was no worry, for he could fix anything. (Another myth that would explode around me one day, but not yet, no, happily not yet. Today was taken up with souls.)

My ears stayed cocked at the ready to receive pronouncement from 'Big Holy Hat'.

'You shouldn't trouble yourself with this . . .' Her voice trailed on, and the rest of the conversation is as much a haze now as it was then.

My grannie thought that being a communist was something bad. What if she was right? What upset me was that she was blaming my father for her worrying about our soul thing.

I sat down on the pavement outside my own door to ponder over what I had just heard, though it was as much out of my grasp as the moon. But the thought that stuck uppermost in my childish mind, and was looming large and horrible, had nothing to do with religion or politics.

My grannie maybe didn't like my father! She just pretended she did.

Who would I tell? I couldn't tell my mother. She'd immediately ask me what I was doing under the window 'earwiggin' at whit wiz nothing tae dae weh me'. Worse still, she might report back to my father, and who knows what would happen then?

I was sitting on the pavement turning all this over in my

mind, when my own angel of mercy appeared: 'Hiv you nothin better tae dae than sit starin intae space?'

Auntie Mary stood looking down at me. She had also been in my life since I was born. She was my father's Auntie really. Auntie Mary knew everything. And better still you could tell Auntie Mary things.

'I dinna think meh Grannie likes meh dad.'

'Oh! Eh! . . . Says Wha?

'She did.'

'Whit did she say tae yeh?'

'No tae me. Tae the nun. She's worried aboot oor souls, because she says meh dad's ane o' they communist things.'

By the time I had finished she was sitting down on the pavement beside me.

Well, yehr grannies's right aboot ae thing. Yehr father's a communist right enough. No that that means anything tae you, an naither it should. Whit should concern you is how lucky yeh are tae hae sich a guid father an mither. An no worry aboot whit yeh heard, when yeh shouldn've been listenin in the furst place. BUT . . . Big Fowk kin get it wrang ana yeh ken, even though they believe whit thir sayin'. Jist like you dinna like it if yehr big brither shoves yeh, but yeh stull like im as yehr brither. Is that no right?

Now weh'll jist keep this tae wirsels. It'll be oor secret. Here's a penny early. Niver let on tae the rest o' them, an yeh'll get anither ane afore Eh go.

More secrets.

But the world brightened up considerably. If memory serves me, I just rushed round to the corner shop with my money, and forgot all about 'Big Holy Hat', communist things, and everything else about that conversation.

Auntie Mary was like my father. Once she said she was taking care of something, it was as good as done.

The eavesdropping episode was never ever mentioned again by me, or to me by my grannie, my parents, or Auntie Mary. But I remember not long after it, my grannie kept telling me how good my father was, and how lucky we were to have him, so I guess, looking back now, as we would have said in my neck of the woods, 'words wir had'.

As I grew to adulthood I was to learn of the complex nature of families, how you could love them then feel like murdering one of them (and they me I am sure), all within the space of days. But family wins every time, thanks to my mother and father.

I was also to learn that that although folk can have different opinions and belief systems, it doesn't make one right and the other wrong, it makes us all . . . just different. Apart from, in my mother's opinion, her family: 'Gon get me the ain that's got the perfect family. Apert fae me that is!' And you know what? She actually meant it!

However, here's a lesson I learned, that I have discovered is absolutely part of the human condition.

From that day on, I hated 'Big Holy Hat' because she never 'belonged' to me, so obviously it was alright to blame her.

# GOIN TAE THE SHOPS

When I was wee there were no supermarkets. Come to that there were no help desks, computers or online anything.

The thought that you could get a great big trolley, and 'do' a weekly shop, all in this huge market place, would have made my mother thought she'd gone to 'Messages Heaven'. For in those days you 'went the messages' daily. And who had the money for a massive weekly shop anyway? So, folks shopped at different venues.

The fruit shop used to house all our organic food; we just never knew that it was organic; we would've just eaten it.

When I think about it, the apples and oranges, potatoes, and lots of other stuff were all 'out of shape'. There were no shelves of fruit that looked like the soldiers you get in the supermarkets now.

The fruiterer who owned the shop never used to like folk handling the goods, and would remind my mother: 'If yeh squash it, yeh beh it.' To which my mother would inevitably reply: 'Eh, Eh ken, but if yeh think Eh'm peyin guid money fir spulters then yehr whistlin up a closie.' ('Spulters': ruined fruit to those who lived along at the Sinderins.)

Thus, having upset the fruit shop man, they would make a deal that he showed her the stuff before he bagged it. No customer complaints desk then, just straight for the jugular! However, the fruit shop did sell off the vegetables and fruit that weren't up to scratch quite cheaply, for soup.

When my mother used to send me for the fruit and veggies she'd command me, 'An mind an no let im treh an palm yeh aff weh auld stuff, fir yeh'll jist march right back weh it.' I used to know the fruiterer would be most indignant when I repeated what my mother's instructions were. But repeat them I did! I never had to live with him! So I guess he never did 'treh an palm me aff' for I seldom got sent back.

The baker's shop in my neighbourhood was to die for. Our baker had a shop at the top of a street, adjoining an open pend. The bake house was round the corner.

You could go and stand at the door of 'the bake hoose' and watch the bakers (there were two of them) at work. You could also buy a penny/tuppenny bag of 'endies'. This would be the crusts of the fruits slices, square iced cakes, and such like.

All the lovely aromas wafted from the bake hoose open doors and windows as you walked into the street. My school was just over the wall from the bake house, and at playtime you could sometimes catch the smell as it wafted over the wall.

And the bread! Oh! The bread! And the big crusty rolls. They were my downfall, and are to this day. Nothing beats a great big slice of bread and homemade jam!

Anyway, now I've stopped drooling. Do you remember getting sent for a half loaf that was actually a loaf? We very seldom got just a half loaf, there were too many of us.

We went through bread like 'sna aff a dyke' and one of us had to take a turn of going to the baker's for bread every day.

Our bread was the kind with 'Plehn Geordie' crust at the bottom and 'Curly Kate' crust rounding off the top. Orders from she-who-must-be-obeyed yet again. Rolls had to be 'crispy, but no so it wid brak wir teeth, but no burnt'. Bread had to be 'crusty on the tap, but jist broon on the bottom, an no hae been sittin on the shelf too lang'.

Once again I was forced to relay all this to the woman at the baker's shop counter. She never seemed to get angry, like the fruiterer, she just said, 'Right yeh are,' and up would come this wonderful fresh bread.

We got the bread that was baked in a two-loaf tin. Sometimes, when I felt brave enough and if it was still hot, I would carefully separate the middle of the two loaves and stick my finger into the hole provided, then pick away at the inside of the bread going back up the road home. The size of the hole depended on how brave I felt.

I knew that when my mother cut the bread I would be 'fir it' for 'manglin' the inside of the loaf, but it was well worth it.

I went to the sweetie shop once a week and spent some of my pocket money on whatever was available for the money I had.

My mother used to make tablet, puff candy and stuff like that, but my favourite bought treats were chocolate drops, and chocolate is still my favourite to this day (mores the pity for the waistline).

My sweetie shop had bottles and trays full of goodies, and it was serious stuff picking your weekly job lot.

One of the things I remember about my sweetie shop was the day the sweeties came off the ration, about 1946–47, after the war.

Up until then, being a war baby, I'd only known sweeties needed a coupon before you could get any. My coupon was always for two ounces (a 'D' coupon) or a quarter (an 'E' coupon), and I would have thought all my birthdays had come at once if I'd been given an 'E'.

The worst was unless you had a good sweetie shop you were only allocated so many of these coupons per week/month. If you went through them too quickly then that was just tough luck on you!

My mother was about six months ahead when the sweeties came off the ration, for she was always stuck for sweetie coupons. At Christmas, high-days and holidays, she would beg the sweetie shop man to let her go onto next month's sweetie rations. And he always did, so we really made of the deal when coupons were abolished.

The man who had the sweetie shop said to my mother: 'Well thank the Lord fir that. Eh've a tin fuhl o' they daft coupons, an naebody here ever kept tae the richt month anywey. Eh'dve really been in the **** if they'd ever came tae ask tae see my coupon book receipt accounts.'

When the great 'Nae-Coupon-Sweetie-Day' arrived, and we were given an extra penny to go and get some sweeties without a coupon, I can recall asking the man at the counter: 'Yeh've no tae yaze up a the aulders first, hiv yeh?' (My mother had a lot to answer for with this gie-me-nae-aulders thing.)

On being reassured that this was not the case, I think I chose some nougat and a bar of Highland toffee. We got to pick two things to celebrate the 'Nae-Coupon-Sweetie-Day'.

Funnily enough I used to find going to the butcher quite boring. I never liked hearing the whack and thump as he cut up the meat. But I loved getting a taste of anything that was going, especially the corned beef.

What did amaze me was that the butcher could walk around like he'd just finished dissecting Frankenstein's Monster and not give a whit!

And I quite liked watching him whiz away as he sharpened up his knife.

The fish shop was a smashing place though, but a bit smelly. It was all white coats, plastic overalls, water and wellies. They had mermaid tiles on the walls. And the one we went to had water running down the window. When I was a kid I used to think the water came up the road from the river (Tay), washed down the fish shop mans window, then weeched right down back into the river.

They practically gutted and cleaned the fish as you waited. I loved the fish shop because there always seemed to be a great deal going on there. And I loved fish! There weren't so many varieties in those days because most folk stuck to filleted haddock and cod. We sometimes had crab, but my father's pal caught them, so we never bought them at the fish shop.

What I *didn't* like was when my Grannie would send me for a bag of cat fish. No, she didn't have a penchance for fancy fish. It was just a bag of fish leftovers for her cat.

The fish man used to keep all the fish leftovers in a box, and just throw some in a bag. I never ever looked into that bag I can tell you, here's to what the bag contained. But my grannie's cat gnawed its way through anything, and that was alright, for the cat never knew it wasn't a filleted haddock.

# SHELTERS, COALMEN,
# AN FOWK IN ATTICS

The tenement I lived in was five storeys high, including the attic and the ground floor. The four upper storeys were reached by going up the enclosed close that made up the outer wall of my house and climbing up an inside stone staircase, which snaked its way up to the top of the building. There was an outside toilet on each landing, and one on the attic landing.

Our tenement had three open walk ways (pletties). When you'd reached the third plettie, the last set of stairs took you up to the attics. There were four attics at the top of the building and their landing had linoleum on it. When I was a kid I thought this was really posh.

Oh! And as I remember, there was this one woman in our street who had a carpet that nearly fitted her whole ben-the-room. Now that was posh as well!

We used to sling greenie ropes over the railings that lined the sides of the first plettie, and use them as Tarzan ropes, rope trees, and swings.

At one time I've seen as many as five swings all weaving in different directions, and inevitably bumping into each other. As my grannie and my mother's 'ben-the-room windies' faced the back green, we annoyed them the most I suppose, but the only time they ever interfered with the games was if there were any battle cries or broken warrior wailings. Then they'd lean out the window and sort us all out.

I do remember though that when my older brother decided he would be Tarzan in earnest, he threw a rope from the *second* plettie and started to climb down it. A neighbour who lived on the first plettie saw him from her kitchen window and nearly had a stroke (I would imagine) when she saw him dangling there.

She opened her window and let out a yell that would've wakened the folk who were incarcerated in the cemetery up the road!

As a result, when he reached the ground, my mother was standing waiting for him. I bet he wished it could have been one of the lions or crocodiles from a Johnny Weissmuller film instead. That was the end of the second-plettie ropes . . . for a wee while.

We had a shelter at the side of our backies (back drying area if you lived out the Sinderins). It was built there for World War II and didn't get knocked down for ages, so it was commandeered as a 'gang hut' by the kids that lived in our tenement.

My brother told me that the Germans had come up to try and murder all the folk who lived in our street. So a few of us (whoever 'us' was then) went into the shelter and made a noise, and the rest (whoever the rest were then) hid around the greenie. And when the Germans went to see who was in the shelter, we all jumped on them.

'Whit happened tae them?' I enquired.

'They a' run awa an got shot someplace else, but they wir feard tae come back here that's fir sure,' was the reply.

The shelter had a flat roof with the metal funnel sticking out of it. It was used as . . . well, anything you liked really, but mainly for climbing up on, from the side where no one could see you, hoping that you'd get at least a wee while before the building of a thousand 'eyes' reported to your own personal set of 'eyes'. This meant that my mother would come round and stand at the bottom of the shelter and shout up: 'How many times dae yeh hiv tae be telt?' Then: 'Right, get doon here, an when yeh do, yehr fir it.'

'Fir it' could mean a number of things, none of them to your liking, so there was really no incentive to come down in a hurry. Then: 'Right! Eh'm gonna coont tae ten . . . ONE. An if yehr no doon beh then . . . TWO. Eh'm comin up . . . THREE.'

I never found out if my mother could have got up to the roof of the shelter. I bet she couldn't, but then again what if she did? And that's what I didn't want to find out.

I always wanted to be one of the gang that went into the shelter, but was always told 'yehr too wee'. I think it was because they used to go in there and light a wee fire with matches they'd nicked from somebody's house. But they always got caught in the end when the smoke came out of the funnel.

We were never out of trouble because of that shelter.

There was also a row of wooden sheds that were fixed on to the mill wall that our tenement joined. We were definably in trouble if we were seen up there, as one lad had fallen through and broken his leg. If I heard once, I heard a million times:

'Dae yeh want tae be like that wee laddie alang the road that broke eez leg. An you might brak baith legs, an then whit? Yehr far too big tae be cerried aboot, so yeh'd jist hae tae bide in the hoose until yeh wir better.'

So no pressure there then. And since 'bidin in the hoose', even when it snowed or rained, was a threat worse than death to me, it was absolutely no hassle to keep away from the sheds.

But one of my uncles had a great use for climbing up onto the roof of the sheds. He worked in the mill next door, and if he slept in, he'd just wait a while, then climb up onto the sheds, walk along the mill wall, drop over and just walk into the work shed as if he'd already passed the front door. I bet he didn't like it one bit when they introduced clocking in.

Now . . . speaking about clocks.

I'd like to tell you about this old woman who lived at the top of our building in one of the attics. I never knew her age; she always seemed about 100 to me.

Every Friday, in the bad weather, when the coalman came to our tenement, she always got a bag of coal delivered to her attic.

I was fascinated by these coalmen. Their faces were always black and streaked, and their eyes shone really white. My mother used to give them a cup of tea after they'd made their deliveries. They would sit on my doorstep, and if you came too near, they made your face all black with coal dust from their hands. They had leather waistcoats, or sacks round their shoulders, and some wore hats with a leather flap that hung down at the back.

These men humphed these great bags of coal on their backs, up all those tenement stairs. If you weren't in, then tough! They left the coal outside your door, and you had to man-handle it into the bunker on your own.

So most folk used to either stay in on the day they'd ordered their coal, or leave their key with somebody else. My mother never worked when we were wee, so sometimes our bunker looked like a locksmith's counter on coal day.

Everyone had a coal bunker in their kitchen, right next to the cooker, and right where you all ate your meals. I used to eat my tea there some nights.

Now there must have been coal dust, but I can't recall ever

noticing this, but my mother was never done cleaning, and that's maybe one of the reasons.

It was when the coalmen were having their fly-cup that I would overhear them speaking about the 'auld ane' up in the attic. I heard by ear-wigging, things I couldn't understand:

'But then, it'll come tae us a,' or 'Puir auld sowel, she's on erh own. An Eh suppose at her age yehr bound tae get a wee buht mixed up.'

Apparently she had a really unusual neighbour (although she just looked like everybody else to me), but this woman was 'worth erh weicht in gold'.

My mother used to hand up a bowl of soup to this old lady once a week. And as I am aware, there wasn't much social care to speak of, so old folk who were on their own did depend on their neighbours.

When I look back, I think the Good Fairy gave my mother that soup pot, for it seemed to be bottomless, and well able to feed the 40,000. She used to say: 'Yeh think Houdini's a magician, wait tull yeh see how far your mither kin eek oot this pot o' soup!'

Anyway. Back to the coalmen.

They told my mother that the 'the auld ane' had taken to keeping all the wee bits of dross from last week's bag of coal, and as she heard them coming along the landing she would run out and pile the wee bits of coal on the landing telling them that, 'They'd better no hae brought any o' that rubbish this week, or they'd get the same again.' Then because she thought she'd been cheated, she used to dock a few pennies of the money she was due, telling the coalman, who only delivered the stuff, 'tae whistle fir the rest!' And after all these insults, she would give the coalman a few sweeties 'fir him an eez pals'.

They used to laugh and say to my mother: 'She's maybe

getting a wee buht forgetful, but erh marbles are still rattlin aroond in there, fir she aye gits erh coal at least tuppence cheaper than anybody else.'

And then she took a liking for the clock tower.

We had a church with a clock tower that was three streets away, but you could see the steeple and hear it chiming the hour in our street.

The auld woman in the attic decided that she would start coming out onto the top plettie whenever she felt like it, and clapping her hands to the hourly chimes. She would follow that by shouting out the correct time so loud that the whole place could hear her.

This didn't seem to upset anyone too much until she decided to sometimes get up through the night and give a running commentary on what time it was.

I remember my father commenting one time: 'Sometime's that ane's jist like haein a great big bliddy cuckoo clock on the tap o' the building.'

I would like to tell you the end of the woman in the attic story, but I can't remember what happened to her.

It's like a whole host of other events that are often part of your childhood, that just vanish in the haze of reaching adulthood.

I hope wherever she landed up they had big clocks and coalmen.

# THE HOOSE GETS
# EVEN MAIR FUHL

My young sister (the bairn) was born on the 22 December. There wasn't going to be enough room for 'her' in our house, even I knew that. But nobody had asked me. And now she was here, there was nothing else for it.

But at least my mother would be coming home soon. She'd only the lead-up to Christmas Day with us. I couldn't believe that. My eldest sister had been appointed second-in-command. I couldn't believe that either. Only my mother or father could be real leaders, but she was the oldest and would be helping out it would seem. But the very worst bit was the week before Christmas.

We (my younger brother and I) were shipped off to my Auntie Mary's when my mother went into hospital. And that was another thing. She didn't have to go into hospital with my wee brother, so what was so special about this one?

So around the 20th December we arrived at Hill Street. My mother would be spending Christmas in hospital with 'the new arrival'. Kids didn't get to visit the hospital, so I wouldn't have to pretend I was happy about the whole thing. We would have an early Christmas present according to Auntie Mary. Some hope!

I loved my Auntie Mary to bits, and she did her best to

make the run-up to Christmas Day as good for my brother and me as she possibly could. But then I said to her we'd been left with her just to make room for the 'new bairn', and that was the cause of all the problems, and I didn't like 'it', or want 'it' anyway.

Well . . . Auntie Mary just about had a fit. Did I not realise how lucky I was that Santa was bringing the presents up to her house because my mother had taken the trouble to let him know she wouldn't be at home? Yeh! Right!

Look at my wee brother. Did I see him making a fuss?

Well! Did he ever?

'And most of all,' says she, poking her finger in my direction, 'did I want to upset my mother when I saw her?'

So much for child psychology in those days.

Anyway, now I knew that my opinion on 'the new bairn' might not be in the least popular, I just kept my mouth shut.

Then it happened. It must have been a Thursday or Friday when we arrived at Auntie Mary's and I announced that the Saturday Club Christmas party was on that Saturday, and who was going to take me on the two tram cars to get there and back to attend it?

With our Saturday Club you got a wee book in the lead-up to Christmas and every Saturday you went, you got it stamped. If you had enough stamps then you got into the freebie party they organised for Christmas. You got something to eat, a big caramel and an ice cream. AND . . . you could go up on the stage and sing. Everybody who was anybody at all went to that Saturday 'Do'.

That is, apart from me it would seem. My father wasn't able to come for me. My sister was too busy helping him. My older brother wasn't allowed to come up for me on his own, and Auntie Mary couldn't leave my other brother.

So she informed me. 'Yeh'll jist hae tae gie it a miss this year!'

Gie it a Miss? Gie it a Miss? She never even turned bright blue or anything!

That to me, back then, was just like saying I had impetigo on my head and they were going to shave my hair off, then slap that awful purple stuff all over my bald head, so the whole world knew! Or the nit nurse was going to find something leaping about my not-shaved hair and stick me behind the blackboard so everybody in the world knew that I maybe didn't have impetigo. I had a nit-loupin heid instead!

Not go to the Saturday Club party! Not go!

Auntie Mary warned me: 'Dinnae even think o' performin, thir's enough goin on!'

So I departed ben-the-room (there weren't many places to stomp off to in those days), plunked myself on the wooden stool that sat at the ben-the-room windie, and just huffed for the whole of the time that the party was on.

I remember quite clearly looking at the 'wag-at-the-wa' clock she had on her wall, and counting the minutes from the start of the party to the end of it. With each minute I ate my wee picnic out of the brown paper bag. I chewed on my caramel and I licked my cone. I went up on the stage and sang 'Yes! We Have No Bananas' (my favourite song of the day). In my head I leapt about the picture house gleefully losing yet another hair ribbon!

And I missed my mother!

My father came up for us late afternoon on Boxing Day:

'Wha wants tae come hame an see Ma, an yehr new wee sister?'

'Us,' we yelled, and for me the answer to the first part of that question was true.

So we all trooped over to my house: Auntie Mary, us, my

father, baggage, Christmas presents and all. My mother had sent a 'wee pressie' for us to bring home to my sister. My father gave the present to me, which I duly passed on to my brother.

When I got home the house seemed to be full of folk coming and going, and admiring 'the enemy', and my new mother sat there, just letting everyone else organise her, in our house.

And here, lying in the clothes basket at the end of the bed that sat in the kitchen alcove was the very root of my worries and problems. This wee red squashy-faced bundle. And she was screaming louder than the mill bummer.

I had just known I wasn't going to like her, and I was right. And the racket. How could my Auntie Mary smilingly say 'that's a guid pahr o' lungs yeh've on yeh bonnie lassie'? She must be going deaf.

Well, I'd have none of it. So I took myself off on my own ben-the-room. Now we'd have even less room for us all with her here.

I dumped onto the settee and shook my new Christmas jigsaw out of its box.

I didn't even look up as my mother came in the room.

'Shove up.' She sat down beside me on the settee.

'What? No even a hello?'

'The place is fuhl . . . an yeh wir busy.'

'When wiz Eh too busy fir you?'

'Well, yeh wull be now!'

'Well now, actually . . . that's whit Eh wanted tae speak tae yeh on yehr own fir . . . Eh'm gonna need a guid hand weh this new bairn, fir she'll be a lot o' work until she's up a buht. Eh need somebody Eh kin really depend on. An Eh think yehr the very wummin fir the joab.'

After a moment's silence my mother said to me: 'So whit dae yeh say?'

I just felt her next to me and breathed a sigh of relief.

We sat there in our silence for some more moments, and then she leaned over and began to give me a hand with the new jigsaw.

Life was back to a new normal and I had a new sister.

# THE MOVE TAE FINTRY
# AN THE NEW SKALE

We moved from the West End of Dundee to a new housing scheme called Mains of Fintry (its proper name), Wintry Fintry (its well-earned name), or just plain Fintry (the inevitable).

We had been allocated our 'new hoose' because the youngest member of our family being born put us on the 'overcrowded' list, which meant that we had to be considered for more room.

There were now seven of us, counting my mother and father, so that obviously meant that there were loads of people under that number still living in just two rooms. But in my grandmother's day there was no list at all, so at least it was a big step up on that.

So we set off to Fintry with the rest of the 'overspill' from various parts of Dundee.

We moved on Rabbie Burns' birthday, and I can tell you that's when we knew why it was called Wintry Fintry. My mother went about hugging her coat round her like she was visiting the North Pole, and that was *in* the house.

We had been used to living in an enclosed area, with loads of works, factories, houses, and four of us all bunged up sleeping in one wee room. Then we landed up in the wide open, in a house that was built with steel walls.

I think that winter we all went to bed with more on than we wore outside. It's true when you hear the tales about there being ice on the inside of the windows in Fintry.

My two brothers got allocated the end bedroom because it was the coldest, and it was immediately nick-named 'The Yukon', and we called it that until the day we left. I remember saying to my older brother: 'Yehve got a bedroom weh the same name as that picture that Charlie Chaplin did.'

'Eh', says, he, 'but heez in Hollywood, an only kiddin on.'

The new house was a block of four flats, and we were on a bottom flat, with a garden of our own at the front and a garden we shared with the upstairs neighbour at the back, but you had your own plot for growing vegetables. My father was not too impressed with that thought. We were never going to be the Waltons, but he did have a go when Spring appeared, and involved my mother in the creation of the vegetable garden. Uh-Oh!

He never involved her too much as he dug up the garden at the back, bought packets of whatever, planted them and watered them. Then we all admired his handy work. My father could be a farmer as well. No surprise there then.

One day, when the schools must have been off, she roped me in to 'weed oot the gairden, fir yehr father's done athin up tae now'. So 'weed-oot the gairden' we did. When I enquired what to leave and what to pull: 'Oh! Jist pull up anythin that looks like a weed.'

Okay! So out came nearly everything that my father had planted, along with the weeds. I shall leave it to your imagination what his reaction was when he discovered this. But my mother, ever philosophical, waited (of course) till he left in high dudgeon and said: 'Eh sometimes winder how Eh iver treh tae help that bliddy man!'

Good job he was out of earshot.

And that was the end of our gardening career!

I remember my mother telling me that after we'd all settled, my father and my older sister were working, my older brother was just about to start (or was already at) the trade school, and my wee brother and I were enrolled at the nearest school, and off on that new adventure, when she caught my youngest sister toddling up the 'loaby' (which was now big enough to be called a hall if you were that way inclined). My sister was knocking on all the doors, shouting for my grannie.

My mother said: 'Eh windered whit the hell she wiz daen, then it dawned on me that she stull thought meh mither wiz next door.'

My sister, of course, saw all the doors and since, in her wee life, it was always one door, one family, she assumed that these doors all had people behind them.

My mother and I had a laugh about that. In later years I was to learn of just how much she disliked her 'new hoose', which had its own living room, a kitchen with a clothes boiler, a bathroom, and your own drying green. No fighting over horses at the washie here.

And *that* was the whole problem for her to start with. She was homesick!

When you think that we were only about forty minutes away from where we first stayed that doesn't seem very feasible. But my mother had spent practically her whole life up the West End until then, and in the cul-de-sac where we had last lived since I was born. So, sure she loved her new house, it was just in the wrong place as far as she was concerned. And none of us even knew about this back then.

What we did notice was that after she put my brother and I into school, she would often go back to visit up the West End. This entailed a walk up the Forfar Road to the tram car, lugging my sister and the Tansad, and she must've only been there for a short while when she had to do the same all over again, to be home for us coming in for our lunch.

What I definitely did not know as a kid was that our family doctor had told her to do just that, and to hell with housework, etc. His advice was '*see to*' the family, and make as many trips back to her old home as possible.

Wise man that he was, he knew that she'd only last doing this trip each day until she made new friends, and she did make new, and lasting, friendships with some other women in the street, who came from similar backgrounds, and I suppose felt the same as her.

You'd think we moved to the moon, but in my mother's case she felt like it! Sure she loved the house, and she saw how happy we all were, once we settled down. And, of course, I went back to the West End for the Saturday Cinema Club until I grew out of it (another crucial life event that bit the dust not long after I moved).

But my mother came from a close-knit community (with its warts and all), and of course she missed that, until she formed another one in Fintry.

But me I loved Fintry from the get go.

What's not to love for a kid that used to walk for twenty minutes to see a bit grass, and then suddenly it's just outside my door?

Fintry housing scheme in those days had only a few streets and was built on farmland. There were open spaces as far as your eyes could see. Now we could be John Wayne in earnest, and gallop to our heart's content, and we did!

We played 'kick-the-can', 'Releefoe' (I haven't a clue what that name meant, maybe Relief-Oh! or Really-Foe) and 'Tig' (running around and catching someone out by touching them on the shoulder).

Then there was a game we played using old tin cans. You

got someone to bore holes into the bottom end of the used can, and then threaded string through one can and attached it to another one, giving you long-distance walkie-talkies. This was crucial in the fight against crime, invasion, and spying, to name but a few. You would each run the length of the string, then one of you stuck the can over your ear while the other one yelled down it, and just like magic, you heard each other. Nothing at all to do with the fact that they were only yards away, and yelling loud enough to waken the dead, never mind alert the enemy!

Oh! And if you stood one foot on one can and one foot on the other, pulled up the string to balance you, which hardly ever got you more than three steps without falling off, but there you had a pair of stilts.

Generally diving about, though, was always my favourite thing, and was the game that I dedicated myself to, unstintingly. And now that I had the wide open spaces of Fintry, I was in my element!

My place in the family was between two brothers and up until then I was the one who 'wiz looked efter', by my older brother, and protected from all things I had to be protected from by him.

Now the cycle was changing.

I was the one with the responsibility. I was the big sister to my younger brother, and I had to look out for him. But I don't think he was even a quarter of the bother that I gave my other brother, for even as a kid my wee brother had the knack of getting along with everybody.

When we moved to Fintry there was still a massive building programme going on all around us, and new streets were springing up everywhere.

So began other, new, exciting games called: aggravate the farmer who still lived next door to us and dodge the workmen and the 'Watchie' (the man who looked after the building site when the day's work was over).

Do you know when I look back I'm sure the Watchies helped me settle into Fintry, because in my heart I think they replaced the wee man that used to chase me about at the Saturday Cinema Club!

And he followed the same format. If he caught you monkeying around near the building sites, and he eventually found out who you were, then he reported to your head-quarters, and it was dealt with.

Once again, I tried valiantly to follow Big John's advice from some war movie or another: 'If yah keep mo-ovin as fast as yah kin, tha'll never hit a mo-ovin tarr-get.' Which, strictly speaking, John, only happened in the movies, and because you obviously didn't have a mother who could hone in at a speed of knots onto *any* target, moving or otherwise.

And so the new life in Fintry began and we started school. This was never a problem with me, as I usually loved school.

The school I had left behind me must have had at least 200 kids attending it. The school dinners were served up in the school hall which was also huge to me, and we had a Head-mistress who could silence the lot of us with a look. Not as good as my father granted, but then he was a hard act to beat in the 'stop-it-or-else' glower department!

What struck me most about my new school was that they were in the process of putting in electric lights. So we had one or two classrooms with big brass lights that pulled down from the ceiling and had to be lit by the teacher.

I was walked most of the road to this new school by my mother, because it was a distance away. In the old place we just ran out the street and into the school.

They had two age groups in one classroom, something else I'd never encountered.

They even let the kids who went 'tattie-howkin' come into school after they'd been up really early picking those potatoes. They never appeared in their old clothes, or anything like that, but they must've been knackered by the time the school came out.

But here's a thing that never changed at all!

In my days they must have had a special part of the training college that turned out nothing but 'Heidies', and they were all act-alikes. The head teacher at my new school treated us exactly like the head teacher at my old school. They both must have taken a special course in 'obey-me-or-else-yeh'll rue-the-day!'

But the big bonus in the new school was the playground. It was a sloping grass hill, and the road along to the school had a burn running alongside it ('stey oot o' there or else') which we duly threw sticks into, and went as near to the edge as possible, threw a rope over a tree and swung out over the water and back. And, of course, missed the bank and jumped into the water, and then had to go home with only wet feet, socks and shoes, if you were lucky.

I grew to love the new school every bit as much as my old one and it was there that I got my first sighting of television.

One of our teachers had bought herself a television, and she was taking us up to her house, in her car, so many at a time. On the day it was my turn I was beside myself with excitement. School ended and off we went up to her house.

When we got there she had made up sandwiches and wee goodies laid out on a long coffee table, all ready for us, and we ate them as we watched that children's newsreel with the rooster that crowed as it spun round. Then we watched some programme about animals, and then *Muffin the Mule*, then she delivered us back home. When you think of it, that woman did that for a class that must have held at least thirty-five to forty kids, so wasn't that a really kind thing to do?

Anyway, when I got home my Auntie Mary was in, and I started on right away. I described the television, which was one of these wee square screens housed in a walnut case of some kind.

But what had really set me sky high was the fact that you could get the cinema right in your living room. Imagine that (I have always loved the cinema). And you just sat there, and it was just for you. I must have babbled on and on, until my Auntie Mary interrupted: 'Awa yeh go! It'll niver tak on. Wha the hell wants the pictures showin in thir hoose night and day?'

Everything I'd been ranting on about had obviously been wasted on her! But worse was yet to come.

As soon as my father appeared from his work off I went again. Now he loved the wireless, so he'd obviously love this new fangled thing? Wrong!!

'Eh than then whit? Diz abody jist sit an stare at this wee box? When dae yeh speak tae ane anither, read a book, gae oot an play . . . etc. etc. etc?'

But they did say they were glad I'd had such a good time. And anyway televisions were that expensive at that time that it never raised the question of whether we should get one or not.

With the passing of a few years, that changed of course, and my mother got so sick of us asking if we could go to so-and-so's to watch the television, that she worked on my father and he relented and we got a television.

On the big day it arrived he told us all that we'd only be watching at certain times, and we did. Then it got switched off and we went and did other things.

When they first introduced films on the television we used

to applaud and cheer at the end of the film, just like in the cinema (here's to what the passersby thought was going on).

I leave the last word on television to my father, who like us all succumbed in the end, because they introduced sport. But he always said that half the stuff they put on television was a load of excrement (or words to that effect). And that was before now, when new televisions have hundreds of stations. He'd say to us: 'If yeh watch enough o' that box, it'll turn yehr brehns tae mush. It's only bliddy electronic wa-paper.'

And so we all eventually settled into life in Fintry.

# FERMERS, WORKIES AN PIECES IN JAM

For quite a few years after we moved to Fintry there was a working farm practically at the end of our road, and it remained there until it was purchased for building more new houses on.

So, for the first few years, there was building work going on all over the place, and never mind Health and Safety; here was a whole new ball game as far as playing went.

During the weekends or school holidays we'd set out for each adventure, my mother's words going in one ear and out the other: 'Bide awa fae they foundations, if a that the earth tumbles doon on yeh, yeh'll be suffocated.'

Who knew back then that you could traumatise your children with thoughts of choking to death? If they did they never told my mother:

Dinna go runnin in an oot o' they empty hooses, thir fuhl o' nails and shavins an Goad knows whit else.

Dinna aggravate the Watchie, an annoy the workies, or anybody else fir that metter.

Look efter yehr brither.

Bide whaur if Eh shout yeh kin hear me an come in.

Bide aff the road fir they lahrries goin in an oot the site.

Jist play aboot an enjoy yehrsels.

Okey-dokey! Off we went.

Had we obeyed all these orders we'd been as well at home, but luckily, like all kids, then and now, we had selective hearing and translated that into:

Dinna get caught runnin roond the foundations, or the empty hooses.

Dodge the Watchie because if he catches yeh yeh'll be fir it when yeh get hame.

Apart from definitely trying not to get suffocated, the one we did have to pay strict attention to was the stay where you can hear me if I shout. Because if she did shout on you and you'd just roamed out of earshot then that was a big no-no.

The only consolation there was that my mother, who was four feet ten inches her stocking soles, had the shout of a seven-foot Viking, so the range you got to roam was quite large.

When she wanted to check up on us, or call us in for something to eat (if we hadn't descended on her first, shouting 'Eh'm stervin'), she would stand up on the window sill in the living room, open the window and yell each of our names in succession.

My father used to say my mother had a voice that could be heard for miles when she was shouting. No disagreement there. We were the ones who had to listen for it.

If you didn't answer back, within minutes, then she was out looking for you, and that was another big no-no. Window sill conversations held with my mother:

'MAMMMIIEEEE.'

I'd run from wherever I was and yell back:

'Eh'm here.'

'Hiv yeh got yehr brither weh yeh?'

'Yeh, heez here ana.'

If he wasn't, the window sill conversation was held all over again with him from wherever he was. She'd continue:

'Come in fir yehr denner in fehve meenits (or alternatively, NOW).'

'Right.'

'Fehve meenits mind.'

'Right yeh are.'

When I think of it, this clocking in went on all the time, at regular intervals, and I suppose it went on with our neighbours as well, because kids I used to play with would suddenly disappear 'aff the geme'.

The more I picture it, once I moved to Fintry and the arena got much bigger, I must have had to train my ears to be on permanent alert, and scope the airwaves like radar.

On this particular day, while we were playing round about some of the houses that were getting built practically at the end of our garden, we met a squad of Glasgow workmen, and my wee brother got his first job. He would be about seven at the time.

My brother and I used to stand on the grass at the back of our house and watch the joiners who were there at work, and we'd watch the houses go up bit by bit, like a giant Lego land.

We were standing eating a piece-in-jam and one of the workies waved at us: 'Gonnae geez a bite o' yehr piece.' That would be a no! So I suppose we just looked at him.

'Gonnae ask yehr Maw if Eh could get a piece as well then?' And I said, 'Yes.' And we went home to ask.

Now I don't know if the man was joking or not, but when I told my mother I remember her looking out the kitchen window: 'Och Eh suppose Eh kid easily gie them a piece.'

My mother would have given the world and his wife a piece. So saying, she dished up two slices of bread and jam, and off we went back to the window of the house they're working in: 'Here yeh are.'

Then there was a shout of another voice:

'That's only two, an there's four o' us.'

'OK. Eh'll ask aghen.' We go to trot off back home.

'Could you ask yehr Maw if she'd bile a kettle as well?'

'OK.' Off we went with the request.

'Oh fir Goad's sake. They might as well come ower here fir thir tea break.'

And that's how, one day during my summer holidays I think it was, four Glasgow workmen came to be sitting on my mother's back doorstep eating bread and jam and drinking tea. And that started the 'workies'-doorstep-piece-in-jam-cup-o'-tea' interludes.

If my father was in they would talk about the time he worked in Glasgow during the war, and he would ask about the building going on. And he would tell them some of the one million and one stories about 'The Yaird'.

And that was how my wee brother got his first job.

Most of the time one of them would come over when they needed a kettle boiled. Then, if the weather was good, they would sit on the doorstep, but if it wasn't they would take the kettle back to the house they were working in.

If we were there, my brother would walk back with whoever had the kettle, and then bring it back home. My youngest brother was always quite shy, but I remember him being the one that wanted to bring back the kettle.

One day he came home and said he'd been given the job of bringing the kettle back all the time, and that they were going to pay him at the end of the week, on Friday, just like them, and when they got their pay, he'd get his.

Now normally this would not have been allowed that he accept money from anyone, but I guess by this time they knew my parents, and my parents knew them.

I remember in later years, when this episode cropped up in conversation, my mother said that these men were working in Dundee because work was scarce where they lived in Glasgow, so they had lodgings here from Monday to Friday, and then went home at the weekends.

One of the guys apparently had a wee lad just about my brother's age, and she guessed he missed him and semi-adopted my brother.

Anyway, from then on in when my brother was off school he would come home on Friday with a real pay packet (they must have got it from someone who made up the wages) and it would have a small amount of money in it. But I remember him being tickled pink that he got a wage packet. When I think about it he must have been the youngest kettle carrier in Dundee.

As I write these memories it keeps coming back to me that we lived in a more innocent time. I also think it's much harder on the young folks nowadays. Of course, you guarded your kids closely back then as well from the dangers that are always there, but I think people became friends more easily, and then they could suss one another out and find out who to trust. For everybody knew the 'Gleskie workies' that were working on the building site. And folk would stop and pass the time of day with them, and they with us, when they could.

Then the houses at the back of my house were built and the Gleskie workies went home.

But we still had many a happy hour to find new empty spaces and houses. Swinging round the lower rails of the scaffolding that surrounded the new houses became a favourite pastime. We must have looked like monkeys in a zoo. So all was well.

Apart from the Watchies that is.

I used to think that Watchies' jobs were to chase kids away the minute they spotted them, and no matter where they found them. All you had to do was be there. And it was the same, be they jute mill Watchies, Parkies (Corporation park attendants if you had a posh park), or building site Watchies.

It never dawned on me they were there to keep watch over the site, or the mill, from thieves or whatever. I thought these guys were there to blight my life!

And another thing. I used to *think* my mother had eyes in the back of her head, but the minute I became involved with Watchies, I knew *they* definitely did!

You'd only to appear within ten feet of wherever, when he'd jump up out of fresh air or shake a fist at you from across a distant spot that was empty a minute beforehand: 'Get goin. Go on. Eh'm no haen any o' your monkeyshines here. Get oot o' here.'

So the only way to combat this was to grow your own extra set of eyes and ears, and that's what we did. If you were playing on the building site and someone else spied the Watchie then cries of 'here's the Watchie' went round quicker than Apache smoke signals.

But poor man (easily seen I'm an adult now), he had to take down the brick walls we built up, and that were dotted all over the place, and put them back on the pile.

We would take the bricks that were lying around from the huge piles that were stacked all over the place and build houses with their own rooms and kitchens, then bring up our dolls (or even a real bairn if you were me, and had a sister that fitted into a Tansad), and then we'd play 'hoosies'. Or we'd build ramparts like the Alamo and shoot each other from one adobe wall to the other. The place must have looked like an archaeological site with all the half-built bricks scattered all over the site.

Also, with all that space you could get on your bike (literally) and cycle down to the burn that ran not too far away. Or take off to the Den of Mains which was only minutes away and cycle all around there. There wasn't the same amount of traffic on the roads then.

Another new phenomenon that had to be investigated was living with a farm at the end of the street. I had been to Edinburgh Zoo and visited working farms, but here was one of my own.

We soon discovered that it grew wheat (I think) and pea pods, and all things rural.

I mention the wheat because we saw it, to begin with, as something to run through, and run our fingers over, and roll around in, and flatten mercilessly, because that was what the kids in the American films did, and nobody freaked out at them.

We would've adopted a little deer if the farmer had had one, just like the kid in another American film did, apart from the fact that it died, just like Bambi's mother, so we didn't want that (having seen off as many goldfish). When we did first approach the big fence that circled round at the farm, this thing, like a hound of the Baskervilles, came running across the grass towards the fence, and we took off faster than a jet plane with she-who-knew-all's words echoing in our heads:

'Dinna go near the fence, or go intae that ferm up the road.' Well we didn't have to be told that one again.

They used to fill up wee open lorries with pea pods, and the lorries used to sometimes come through our street to get to the main road. If you jumped up and grabbed a handful of peas when the lorry passed by, they used to come off in a trail, and leave you with a whole load of pea pods to wash and enjoy.

When I look back, those farmers must have loved us.

Oh! The one thing that we did get from the farm, that I wanted nothing to do with, was horse manure. I used to vanish like a dust wind if a horse and cart from the farm came down our street, and my father was at home, or had left word with my mother to 'treh an get some dung fir the gairden'.

So if you were in sight, you got the job of seeing if the horse left any of its calling card in the street. Hence the reason I did my Houdini if I could. It used to 'gie me the boak' shovelling that stuff up into the bucket.

One time, my father the gardener, got on the gab with one of the farmhands from up the road. And that was when the horse's dung story entered our family history book.

He'd been asking this farmhand for gardening tips. Actually, my father got quite interested in his garden and we did eat potatoes, cabbages, turnips, carrots and lettuce that he grew. And rhubarb, which made great crumble.

So anyway, he'd apparently got this guy's advice that, as the ground we were on was quite good, the only thing we need do was to put horse manure on top of everything and it would grow perfectly.

Good plan. Could he (my father the gardener) get some from the farmhand, instead of just collecting it in a bucket when, and if, the horses passed?

'No problem,' says the farmhand. He would get us some and deliver it right to the door. So my dad gave him 'a wee bung' for his trouble and we waited on the horse manure.

We didn't have to wait long!

A couple of days or so later, we, and surrounding

neighbours, were wakened to this most awful smell that would've made your toes curl up. When this was investigated, there, sitting on the road in front of our house, was . . . a cartload of horse manure.

That farmhand must've given every horse on the farm a cure for constipation the night before. There was enough in that pile for the whole street. So that's what happened. Everybody just helped themselves to the 'bounty'.

I leave the last word on this one to my mother, who I don't think ever really saw the point of growing your own stuff (and yes it maybe does taste better) when a wee mannie in a fruit shop could just take your order and get *his* hands dirty. Her comment on the mountain outside the front door: 'It's the furst time Eh've peyed money fir a real pile o' . . . . .'

Answers please on a postcard!

And my very last escapade as a farmer was when I went to the 'tatties'.

The fact that I got there at all was a miracle in itself.

When I was just up at secondary school they used to let you have time off to harvest the potatoes for the farmers. I think it was three weeks you got. So when I got the parent authorisation application form home, I was in seventh heaven about getting to go and earn some money with my pal and the rest of the school. But as I went home, deep down in my heart, there was a warning bell ringing away.

My father had other ideas and that was no surprise to me, for I'd lived in the same house as him all my life: 'Thir'll be nae cheap labour oot o' this hoose' seemed to sound the death knell on the extra school holiday.

I was subsequently treated to a lecture on how 'they' – the farmers – and 'they' – the Government – should pay someone who was out of work at the moment the right wages for the job, and not enlist children.

I said nothing. I knew a real brick wall when I saw one. So where was there a chink in the wall?

'Eh'll be the only ain in meh class no goin, an Eh'll be stuck in some ither class weh fowk Eh dinna even ken, or some coarner, until it's a ower. Meh pal's goin. She's getting tae go. Abody but me's gettin tae go.'

'Enough,' commanded my mother, although I think she really meant 'mercy'. 'Gie me that form. Lahve it weh me. An not anither word aboot it or else yeh'll be goin nowhere if ee hears yeh.'

Some days later I got the verdict delivered. I was indeed getting to 'gae tae the tatties'. However, I was definitely not getting to go to a private farm even though it was much better wages. I'd have worked for nothing by this time but had the sense not to say this. I was only going if it was with the school. Less money indeed, but a supervisor was appointed with each bus to look after us. I had a shorter working day. You were allocated a school dinner that was served up at the local school in that area (they were pretty awful in my opinion). The bus picked you up at the school and dropped you back off at the same place. I was not to moan if I was tired or had a sore back.

And last, but by no means least, I was not to see this as a sign that anybody (my father in other words) had given in, but as a special favour to me. This would be treated like all requests, on their merits.

There was no danger that I'd rock the boat. I was getting to go to the 'tatties'.

As usual, my mother had dealt with everything in her own way.

Before I set off to be a farmer in real life, she made me a wee bag on a string to put my money in when I was paid at the end of each day. My daily wage was eleven shillings and thruppence.

I was instructed to stick the bag down my jumper so it would be safe and I wouldn't lose it.

My mother packed me grub to eat whether I got a dinner or not, after I'd said the dinners were rubbish. She got up early and nipped across to the wee shoppie that sold fresh rolls to make up my 'pieces'. She made sure I had on thick socks and had gloves, and was well wrapped up for the day's work.

Then, she gave me her orders for the allocation of potatoes we got to take home after each day, called a 'bilin' [boiling]. But we used to get quite a big bag full that would have done several boilings. Some farmers used to let you fill up the sack as long as you could carry it on the bus. Some days I went back on that bus trying not to stagger under the load of hand-picked spuds I had.

My potato orders were: 'Get some fir chips and some tae mash, a nae rotten ains, feel thir firm.'

You'll notice how working for the farmer came secondary to getting the best potatoes I could to bring home.

I remember my mother getting a clean jam jar, and each evening I put the ten shilling note into the jar, and I got the one shilling and thruppence. It was great watching the jar grow, and for three weeks I was a millionaire with all these extra shillings and thruppences.

At the end of the three weeks we counted the money and decided what it would be spent on. I think it would be school stuff for my brother and me, and some goodies for us as well!

Oh! There is an add-on to the potato saga.

When I was at the big school later on we did needlework in one of the classes. What's that got to do with potatoes? Well . . . at one of these classes we made knickers out of blue material with tiny flowers on it. The pattern was one of these 'fit any size' things, and the knickers I made would've fit anybody right enough. My mother just shook her head and threw them in some drawer.

Anyway, I came home one night during my stint at the 'tatties' to find my school-made knickers hanging from a hook in the wee 'back loaby' that led out into the back garden, filled with . . . yes, potatoes.

My mother had sewn up the bottom of the legs, cut a hole in the waist and pulled through the elastic that was threaded there, tied the elastic in a knot and made my knickers into a bag for holding the big chip potatoes so that they wouldn't get all bashed and bruised.

And that's just what my cornflower-blue coloured knickers (with rosebuds on) did until they turned into a duster.

And so life in Fintry carried me forward from childhood into adulthood.

I left school and began my working life from Fintry, which was now turning from the four or five streets that I had moved to into the sprawling housing development that it is now.

Both houses that we had in Fintry stand to this day.

Eventually, all the spaces we ran around in grew smaller.

And we all grew up.

# GOIN TAE THE BIG SKALE
## AN GETTIN SENSIBLE

One of the worst things you could have said to me when I was just entering my teens was the word 'sensible'. I'm not all that sure I like it much now. It's akin to 'responsible'. None of the two of them ever add up to a night of abandonment and fun.

I had been living in Fintry for about three years now and another 'Big Day' was coming up.

The seven-weekies were nearly over and I had left the primary school and I was 'gaen up tae the 'big skale''. Being a real kid was very nearly over.

In the 'big skale' I had to take charge of a new type of book called a timetable and I was to organise my own homework and, had I but known it, sort out the million and one books I was about to acquire. When I think on it timetables at school are the precursor to schedules at work.

I also had a new uniform, a new grown-up school bag, and a new feeling of excitement and anxiety that I'd never experienced before.

Oh! I was looking forward to going to the new school right enough, since I would know some of the girls who left primary with me, and going on the bus on my own was something I'd done before, but this was uncharted waters right enough.

I got the choice to stay at school dinners when I wanted, but I can say here that I only stayed at the school dinners if I had to. I liked going on the school bus, so to experience it four times a day instead of just two suited me fine. Even if it meant diving off the bus at lunchtime, running up the street like a whippet, burning my mouth by not blowing on the hot soup long enough, and eating the rest of my dinner (lunch now) as I ran back to the bus.

Looking back now I think the bus, for me, became a mobile version of the cinema club when I was wee. The conductors who ran these buses did just that:

'Come on.'

'Shove up the bus.'

'Nane o' that monkeyin aboot.'

'Get aff.'

**'Tak yehr turn.'**

'Right you. Eh've hid enough . . . You . . . **GETTT AFFFF!!**'

And 'GETTT AFFFF' you did, before they threw you off. Worst of all was if the conductor was somebody that knew your mother then you ran the danger of them telling on you.

If it was a big lad (or lads) that caused the trouble, and it was a clippie, then she'd *ding-ding-ding* that bell until the driver stopped got out his cab and came and sorted it out. That got the assembled mass diving for the nearest seats.

There were early buses that could get me to school in plenty time, but like the rest of the kids in Fintry I wanted to get the one and only bus that dropped me off at the school about ten minutes before I had to start.

We used to queue up for that bus in a bundled noisy mass of books and school gear, then the bus came, and it was every man for himself. No big brothers with me now to step in. Then sometimes, you'd get right up to the bus, and the hand that should have had 'verboten' tattooed on it would shoot out: 'Sorry. That's it! The bus is fuhl up.'

Well that was true when you looked at all the squashed sardines that were fortunate to be on, so what was one more. I'd give it one more try and depending on how pitiful, or desperate, I looked, it either worked or it didn't. And that was the difference between detention and no detention.

If you didn't make the school hall before the bell stopped ringing then one of the gatekeepers (teachers in real life) marked a book with your name and class and you either got lines or detention.

And I never bothered moaning about being late to my mother because not only did I not get any sympathy I just got:

'Well serves yeh right. Yeh should get up when yehr shouted on, an get an earlier bus. Eh'm fed up seein yeh runnin oot o' here like yehr on fire.'

I attended an all-girls' school. Assembly was in the main hall of the building, and the head teacher of our school certainly knew the meaning of the words sensible and respon-sible. This woman took no prisoners.

I think there must have been round about 300–400 girls at the school, so you can picture the noise as we all gathered for assembly. Then the whole place faded into silence, and you knew the 'Heidie' had just walked into the hall. This woman silenced us all by just being there.

I think I was only once reported to her, and I can't remem-ber what it was for now (honest). I think it was something to do with yakking going up the stairs. But the wait outside her office door until the buzzer went to summon me in lasted all week in my head. And when she was finished with me, the talking-to she gave me made sure I never went back.

And so I began to learn about having the right books for the right days, keeping up with my homework myself, and I settled in to the secondary school, and I loved it most of the time!

One of the classes I opted to go to was called Housewifery, now known as Domestic Science or Home Economics. It was there that I learned my mother couldn't iron properly.

We'd to bring in a pair of socks and a hankie to the school, which we duly washed and ironed. Well, first of all my mother *never* ironed socks. They just got rolled up together and you stuck them in the drawer. Wrong! She should have been ironing them from the top to the toe and then folding them.

The hankie was even worse. You should've ironed round all the sides, then folded it in half and pressed that, then folded it again, then ironed that, then one last half fold, and it was done. Okey-dokey!

Now, considering I'd lived in my house all my life you would think I would have learned, but to this day I sometimes don't see the brick wall that's in front of me. So on that basis, I waltzed home from school with the 'professionally finished' socks and hankie and informed my mother that we'd been 'daen them a wrang' and:

'Eh could show yeh how tae iron they hunkies the right wey.'

'Oh! Could you now?'

'Yup.'

And with that I proceeded to go through the whole palaver in mime, using my finished articles, and at the end proudly displayed them.

'How much o' a family diz this wummen hae.'

'Eh couldna tell yeh.'

'Well Eh could tell you. No as much as me. An if you've

time tae muck aboot ironin weh jist the one hunkie, then get ehr tae show yeh how tae iron shirts, and you kin iron a pile o' them fir me.'

I should have known that a woman who could turn my blue knickers with rosebuds on them into a tattie bag would have no time for the finer intricacies of ironing.

Another episode was when I brought home a pudding they called something like 'Iced Snow' that I made in one of the housewifery cooking classes.

My mother wasn't in, but my older brother was, and when I put the Iced Snow down on the table his first comment of: 'Jeezie Peeps wha's gonna eat that rubbish? The bottom o' it's a green?' set it all off.

After he'd made a fool of my efforts for some time I got fed up, marched into the bathroom and plunked the whole lot down the toilet. It promptly bunged up the toilet, much to my brother's delight, who was then nearly rolling on the floor. If that wasn't proving his point then nothing could.

But disaster once more! We couldn't flush it away, no matter what we did. It was well and truly stuck. It not only wouldn't go down, it wouldn't come up either.

So he then took pity on me and set about trying to get it out of the toilet. But I think the word 'Iced' should have had 'berg' tagged on the end, and 'Snow' meant avalanche.

My mother arrived home. She couldn't shift it. 'Yehr father's gonna be well pleased at this when ee gets hame.' I don't think the bookie would've taken any odds on that being true.

So, after he did arrive home and got informed of what had happened, he eventually got it moved with some tool he had in his toolbox. While I got: 'If yeh've got any brehns now's the time tae start yazin them.'

Here we go again with sensible and responsible. But the toilet got unstuck and the words Iced Snow were never heard again.

I loved some of the new subjects like science and history, but hated geography and maths (still do). But most of all I fell in love with being my own boss for the first time, and, yes, learning to be responsible.

It was at secondary school that I joined the literary class and learned to love Shakespeare and poetry as much as *Just William* and *Treasure Island*.

I learned that the days of being spoon-fed, as far as school went, were over. And more importantly learned that with words like 'responsibility' and 'sensible' came another big word – 'freedom' – to be your own boss in a lot of ways (as long as I remembered who the real bosses were when I got home).

And here was a surprise bonus that I was completely unaware of when I first walked through the doors of my secondary school. There was a boys' school not more than two minutes away in the next street.

* * *

However, I have rules about the responsible/sensible code. I treat it like I treated the 'Promise' at the cinema club when I was wee.

When I feel like it all bets are off! Then I go and do something that's neither, like try to write a book or something else that lets me know I'm still alive and kicking.

# THE PEH AFF THE
# LID O' THE BOX

Every week we always had 'pehs an bridies' for our dinner on Saturday. This was normal practice for many Dundee families. Lunchtime was called 'dinnertime' back then.

I used to go with my mother to help her carry the shopping home on Saturdays. We followed the same route every week: Keiller's first for the pies, Wallace's next for the bridies and the chocolate duchess cake, then the rest of 'the messages', and back home on the bus.

One of life's embarrassing moments for me was one Saturday when we were waiting in the queue at the bus stop to get the bus home. The queue was full of replicas of us, all loaded down with bags, and it was about a mile long, as was the usual on Saturday.

My mother was giving me the: 'They'll a be stervin in the hoose an chompin at the bit – Eh hate this melee at the Seturday bus stop. Dinna let anybody bash that bag fir you've got the Duchess cake in it.' And all this without even a glance at me or drawing breath, as she carried on a conversation with the woman next to her in the queue.

So anyway, the bus finally appears. We could see it was full and didn't know if we'd have to wait for the next one. So we all took up our stance and made ready to ensure 'naebody gets in front o' us'.

We'd made it right up to the bus when the conductress uttered the dreaded words: 'Wir fuhl. Next bus!' accompanied with sticking her hand up in a Gestapo salute that brooked no argument.

She looked up the bus to check if she could squeeze anyone one else on, looks at my mother and says: 'Right, shove yehrsel on, missus!' Which my mother duly did.

Then quick as a whippet the clippie sticks her hand up in front of me: 'Fuhl up! Wir fuhl up!' *ding-dings* the bell and the bus took off, leaving me on the pavement.

The first thought in my head was I'd no money and would have to walk home with the bags if I couldn't see anybody in the bus queue that I knew.

Then my mother's shout, which must've been heard in China, got everybody's attention including mine: 'Stop this bus right now! Meh lassies left on the pavement weh the bridies an the Duchess cake fir wir dehnner. Eh'm tellin yeh! Stop this bus!' To my amazement (and I would imagine half the queue's) the bus conductress promptly pushed the bell at least four times and the bus ground to a halt. 'Hurry up!' commands my mother, hanging off the back of the bus. 'Get on so weh kin a get hame!'

Even in my embarrassment as I jumped on the bus, I was well impressed. My mother had taken charge of the bus and, more importantly, issued the conductress with her orders for a change. My hero!

The conductress had the last word though as she crammed me into the bus as it took off. She gave me a shove: 'Next time, you jump on quicker, or Eh'll *no* come back fir yeh.'

I have never been so glad my mother was taken up with relating the saga to someone she knew on the bus!

* * *

My father always got a whole bridie and a pie, and we got a pie and half a bridie. My mother usually ate on the trot, as she ran round serving everyone else.

Keiller's pies were the best. They came in a long box to keep them from breaking, and there were six pies to a box, with a juicy pie picture on the lid.

I remember, when I was younger, some kid at school telling me that Keiller's saved money by getting cheap kangaroo meat from Australia, and sticking that in their pies (his mother must've liked Wallace's pies better). Apparently, if you ate too many Keiller's pies, you started jumping about all over the place, couldn't stop and jumped forever.

When I related this might happen to any of us to my mother, she dismissed it with:

Whit a load o' tripe! If yeh wid pey as much attention tae whit the teacher says, as you dae tae whit half they stupit numpties in yehr class tell yeh, yeh'd be the tap o' the class. An as fir the jumpin a ower the place, well then thir's nae change there, is thir?

Fair enough! I was never, ever, convinced as a kid, about the kangaroo thing though, no matter what my mother said, but I scoffed the pies anyway and just chanced it. They always tasted great, and I never started *boing-boinging* along the street, so that was fine.

The picture on top of the box of pies displayed a pie with a quarter section cut out. This allowed you to see how much mince was inside (kangaroo or otherwise), and also showed there was no fat in Keiller's pies, and obviously only the very best of mince.

But that pie on the lid of the box served another purpose in my house.

Some weeks, one of us had to take a turn of getting the 'peh aff the lid o' the box'. The one with the quarter cut away, and as this was always the case, it never struck me as particularly strange.

The reason as far as we knew for the turn-taking was that my mother would cut a section from one of the pies, as they were heating up in the oven, then she would just eat the quarter pie, leaving the remaining pie that looked exactly like the 'peh on the lid o' the box'.

My father never had to take took a turn of 'the three-quarters peh', because, she informed us, he had to go out to work and bring in the money to put the pies on the table in the first place. Seemed only fair, right enough.

So, each time, we duly took our turn of getting three quarters of a pie. And do you know, we never even questioned that she might have another reason for this ritual?

Years later I was to learn that the quarter pie my mother ate was the only pie she ate, along with her half bridie, as we sometimes couldn't afford the extra box of pies that week.

She hid this fact so skillfully we never ever noticed. She was always running around looking after everybody else and never really sat through a whole meal with us anyway.

But on the upside, she used to get the *biggest* slice of the chocolate duchess cake we got out of Wallace's Pie Shop in Castle Street. That suited her fine, for she had a very sweet tooth.

Oh! And I can vouch for that cake being one of the best chocolate cakes I have ever eaten.

Even as an old lady, my mother could not be persuaded to eat more than a small plate full of plain food, saying: 'Goad's truth, Eh'll burst if Eh treh an eat that lot. That plate fuhl's the sehz o' Wattie's denner.'

But put down a plate of fancy cakes in front of her, and you could lay odds on they'd vanish . . . 'jist like sna aff a dyke'.

# THE WOMEN O' DUNDEE
# THAT MADE ME

What is a Hero?

Definition: A person distinguished by courage, decency and fortitude, amongst other things.

When I was writing my memories of where I lived as a child and why I am me really, I decided to put this in with the rest of them, because one day I was reading a story about what makes a hero, and my lot (along with many others) seemed to fit the bill. Or as my mother would've said: 'Eh weh're the hero's yeh niver here o'.' And just give a smile!

'Thank Goad meh plots in the cemetery's up the road, an far enough awa that'll no hae tae lusten tae that bliddy bummer fir ever.' That was something I once heard my grandmother laughingly say, but I think that must've summed up what a lot of them felt back then.

My grandmother had lived in Dundee ninety-odd years, without even having been out of the country. She worked and paid rent all her days and if she'd stolen a brick from the houses she'd lived in for all these years, she could've got turfed out.

She was fed to the mills, like my Great-Auntie Mary, as a child part-time worker, and continued to work until she could retire.

Mill workers in those days toiled from 7 a.m. until 5 p.m., with two short tea breaks, and a thirty-minute break at noon. To facilitate cost productions and profits, they were in the main women. They earned low wages, in mostly dangerous and abysmal conditions. Most jute empires were built on the backs of such labour.

As a child, some of my earliest memories are of the banshee cry of the bummer. It wailed three times. Second time, after fifteen minutes, that meant you were 'quartered' (fifteen minutes off your pay), third time after thirty minutes (you lost thirty minutes pay), and then you could be locked out for the day (no pay for that day at all).

I recall lying there, especially in the winter, thinking how lucky I was that my mother didn't have to join her brother and my grandmother, as they ran along the road to the mill.

My own mother worked in the mills from the time she was thirteen until she had her first child. By the time I came on the scene my mother had the 'luxury' of staying at home because my father had a 'guid joab weh guid pey', apart from when 'The Yaird' was on strike. And this was a common occurrence.

I played in the shadow of a huge mill chimney stack, the mill walls being only about twenty or thirty feet from my door. In my street you mainly worked in the mills (or, men only, in the boatyard, the railways or building sites).

In those days, 'broke' meant you had no money at all, for some folk, not even enough to buy their weeks messages.

I once went with my mother to visit a friend and she took a wee packet of tea, just in case the friend had forgotten to 'get her messages in'.

We always had tea in our house, and plenty food and milk, and more than one shift of clean underwear.

We were given a gift that money couldn't buy. We were taught to respect ourselves and everyone else around us, to know our worth, and to also know that money does not 'maketh the man', but it sure is a handy commodity to have in the world we all inhabit.

My mother brought up five kids on one pay, and had to manage us a lot of the time on her own, for my father was always away to some committee meeting room, or some march, or some demonstration fighting 'the cause'.

But she always said she knew it had to be done, and it was right. She herself was a member of the Labour Party for some years. Her and my Great-Auntie Mary (the suffragette) could provide another story all in itself.

I recall one of my mother's stories about how, during a long strike, my father (and others) would go berry picking to earn some extra money. He would walk to the Carse of Gowrie and back, so they wouldn't be spotted by one of the undercover clerks from the labour exchange if you got on the bus.

If you were caught it meant your money for that week would be cut, and then you might have to be involved with the dreaded 'parish'.

When my father returned home from 'the berries' he would steep his hands in a bowl of water and bleach, so that the 'sign-on' clerk could not see the red berry dye, for then again, you were instantly suspended and lost that week's money.

The 'parish' was for those who were in need, and was apparently one of the most humiliating experiences, and to be avoided if possible. My grandmother used to say she knew why folk committed murder after a visit to 'that place'.

As an adult, my mother never ever had to go there. But I remember my mother telling me that when she was a small child, her own mother was forced, at times, into having to seek what help she could get from the parish. Just like many for other families back in those days, it was a common occurrence.

With the passage of time, conditions improved, but, in the main, only through the struggle and the sheer determination and perseverance on the part of the working classes. Conditions that we take for granted today were fought for by someone before us.

So there you have it, a small insight into some of my own unsung heroes. And there were many more, just like them.

I had the privilege to watch, listen and learn from them, and others like them. They would have laughed in your face if you had told them they were exceptional, for they never even considered that fact.

And because my mother and father, and many others, always had hope and a faith in the future, I, and many others just like me, reaped the rewards.

They had the ability to face up to what life threw at them, and have a laugh at it just the same.

My world now is planets away from theirs, but when writing these memories it's just like old times, and having a good old blether.

It's thanks to all of them that I have most of these stories to tell at all.

# ROABIES

Where I lived when I was a child there was a dance hall down from us in a street called the Well Road. If you are a Dundonian you will have automatically now translated that to Well Roadie.

I am convinced that in the far-off days, Genghis Khan and his hoards once took a holiday in Dundee, hence the 'ie' on the end of almost every word that it can be put on the end of.

When I was fifteen, living in Fintry, I was allowed to 'gae tae Roabies' as long as my older brother was there, and he would be responsible for my safe-keeping when I was let loose in the dancing.

The preparation for 'startin tae go tae Roabies' began earlier than the actual 'Big Day'.

My brother's task to begin with was to keep an eye on me inside the dance hall, and then make sure I got on the bus afterwards. This he did, and then I discovered I could get other escorts to the bus stop that were a lot more interesting than my brother.

Robertson's Dance Hall changed into 'Roabies' somewhere between the 1940s to 1950s. It was about 1955 when I first started going there. By that time it was one of *the* halls for all Dundee jivers.

Learning to jive was to be taken very seriously in my neck of the woods, as the best jivers, with the fanciest footwork, got the most dances.

My older brother and his pals used to descend on my house sometimes, usually over a weekend. If I was lucky then they'd roll back the carpet (not many fitted carpets in these days), and give me personal tuition.

My brother was one of the best jivers I have ever seen. Sure I was biased, but that's a fact! He had a natural movement that made it all look easy, but you had to practice to get good at it, and practice I did.

I would jive with anyone who gave me the least encouragement. I loved it from the word go, and took to it like the proverbial duck.

My best pal would come up to my house and we would practice together. In those days it was not unusual for two girls to jive together, and my pal and I became experts at leading and following.

My mother went bananas because there wasn't a door handle in our house that wasn't loose by the time I was a 'real jiver'. That was because if there was no one to dance with, I would tie a short rope (or one of my nylon stockings) round the door handle and jive with the door, as I tried to perfect all the moves.

Most of the practice took place when my father was out, because I could put the music up louder then. If you put the music up too loud, he'd shout: 'Get that bliddy racket doon, or get it aff.'

Back then I thought it just went to show what a rotten taste in music he had. Nothing to do with he wanted some peace, and if he didn't get it, he took action.

I remember one time when I was upstairs playing Elvis' 'Are You Lonesome Tonight?'

I had bought the record about a week previous, and had played it on the wee gramophone in my bedroom upstairs. I loved that Elvis to bits, so I must have played the record about 100 times, and my father must've had enough. The voice from the bottom of the stairs pronounced: 'If you dinna pit that record aff, you'll be the ane that's lonesome the night.'

Fair enough. I put it off for about an hour, and then in my infinite wisdom (considering I had known my father all my life) I put it on again. First low, then up a wee bit, and so on. By the time I'd finished putting it up and prancing round the room, I didn't hear him until he'd opened the door, marched across the room, picked up the record, cracked it off the top of the gramophone, never even looked at me, marched out with a: 'Well it's aff now.'

I have to say a bit here about Elvis. I was about fourteen when I went absolutely nuts about this guy. I bought as many photos as I could and plastered them all over the bedroom walls, even on the bedroom ceiling and inside the wardrobe. I bought transfers and ironed them onto my tops, the pillow-cases and a cushion.

But there was an Elvis tragedy in my house one day!

I must have 'had words' with my older brother, and when I went out, he up and drew moustaches on practically all of my Elvis posters.

When I came home I went bananas. So big was his crime that I told on him. My father's reaction:

Well, eeh'll jist hae tae replace them, an whit a kerry on aboot some daft bugger that's claim tae fame is he kin shout an jump aboot like an eejit. Look at a' the trouble and stervation in the world . . .

My mother's reaction:

> Eh! Eh ken, but thir no stervin in her bedroom, an he'd (my brother) nae business daen that anyway. But thir baith tae blame, she'd be aggravatin him some wey.

My brother's reaction? Well, we made up, and he bought me some new Elvis stuff.

There was some absolutely classic jazz/rock music to dance to: Elvis, The Clyde Valley Stompers, Bill Haley, Sid Phillips (his was a big band), Humphrey Littleton, just to name a few.

When I look in the mirror now I see this middle-aged woman (I know . . . but I refuse to be an old woman), but in my heart I still see the girl that used to love that music (and still does).

Roabies had an unofficial dress code. The Teddy Boy look had just arrived!

These guys wore coloured suits with a dozen velvet pockets of a different or co-ordinated velvet colour. The shirts were mainly white or black, some of them with gold tips on the collar. The ties were boot-lace, with a fancy ornament which you pulled up to the neck. You could have painted the ceiling without a ladder from some of the platform shoes that the men wore to finish off their outfit. To top this all off was the D. A. haircut.

Elvis Presley had one, but my brother and his pals had one first.

I remember I made a date with this guy who was a real Teddy Boy and had a purple suit, and wore a pink shirt. My father said: 'Dinna bring that object alang the road tae this hoose until efter dark.' He was joking I think, but I never put it to the test.

The girls' uniform was a blouse (preferably with a

mandarin collar), a black straight wrap-over skirt, black stockings with filled-in black heels and a black seam, which could also have ornamentation (butterflies and such like around the heels, if you could afford it), and the mandatory black bopper shoes. These were flat velvet pumps. I remember decorating my boppers with precious stones I had purchased from the open market in the Overgate for about sixpence for a bag of fifty.

I would tie my hair back into a pony tail and stick my sideburns down with a sugar and water mix. This mix kept my sideburns in place no matter how hot it was, or how much jumping about I was doing. Once your sideburns were sugared and watered it was on for the duration, but when it came to taking it off at night, boy did it make your eyes water.

Eye make-up was as outrageous as you wanted it to be.

Dusty Springfield had nothing on me.

I even used to paint one eye with green eye shadow and one eye with purple eye shadow, and then put a strand of purple and green nylon hair through my hair and tie it all in a multi-coloured ponytail. Hair from, yet again, that exclusive boutique, 'the old outside Overgate Market', that was just at the bottom of the West Port.

There used to be a shop at the bottom of the old Overgate that sold all the jiver gear, and it was cheap. So after I had purchased my stuff and learnt to jive, I was literally ready to rock. And I did.

I went for three to four years to Roabies. There were other venues such as the Parker Street Jazz Club and the Continental on Sunday nights. The famous jazz bands all came to the Empress Ballroom in Dundee on Tuesday nights.

Roabies used to run marathons and folk used to jive or dance until there was the 'last man standing'. I never ever went in for that, but I know of folk who did. And so it was I bopped my way through to nearly the end of the '50s.

Come to think about it, I was brought up in a normal working-class home in Dundee, at that time. The man usually worked and brought home most of the money, so he was head of the household. If my father said 'no', then that's what it meant. Not 'maybe', or 'just suit yourself anyway', but '*no*' as in *finito*!

But when I used to get all 'dolled up' in my various rig-outs to go boppin all over the place, his only comments used to be: 'Decided tae jine the circus hiv yeh?' Or some other like phrase. I think basically if I wasn't harming anyone, and not up to any real monkey shines, he just ignored it all (and me as well, I would imagine).

My mother, on the other hand, thought all her family were perfect (smart woman). I always joke that if any of us had been had up for murder, my mother's first words would have been: 'Well, whit did they dae that aggravated yeh as much as a' that?'

When I was nineteen I graduated to The Paliase in Tay Street. I think I graduated to there when I began to get really serious about meeting the other sex. There I learned to waltz, quickstep, and all the other dances that were the order of the day. Once more, you had to be able to dance to ensure you got all your dances.

And so another social ritual began.

* * *

I have always loved to dance. I loved the New Year or weddings when I was a kid, when everybody took you up on the floor and whirled you round. I loved dancing with my feet on top the adults, so that they made the moves and I just floated along on the breeze.

But if I had to choose, I think it would have to be Roabies, which has held a special place in my heart. It was there I began my first true incursion from childhood to adulthood.

And that was what it was, an initiation – a path we all travel, no matter what our road.

I suspect that if you took a night of leaping and bopping at Roabies, and compared it with a frame from a film of a Swahili initiation ritual dance, there would few differences.

In my case, I could have asked for no better compound, or tribe, from which to carry out one of my rites of passage.

# THE REAL WORKER

It was approximately 1956. By this time we'd moved to another house in Fintry, and from our Fintry flat to a house with its 'ain up an doon stairs'.

My wee sister was a young girl now, and the rest of us had, at varying stages, moved into other phases in our lives. My wee brother was now bigger than me now. Not hard to beat I admit.

And now it was my turn, as they say, to put aside such childish things. That has always struck me as a great pity and I tried then, as I do now, to hold onto this child who was once me, for it's her antics that keep me going when I need them.

I had left school and started work in the SCWS in the City Centre some months earlier.

I just thought about something. When I was going to my work I used to put on ankle socks so that I could get on the bus as a half fare, and then take them off again when I got into town. I used to do this whether I was hard up for money for the dancing or whatever (which was the norm for me). Then eventually I suppose the bus driver just said: 'No way! If you're a half fare, then Eh'm a monkey's uncle.'

I also became expert at ironing my older brother's shirts for a small fee, and that also paid me into the dancing for a night.

Money to me was always something to make you happy, or why have it? So no change there then.

While I was working in the SCWS I was going for training at a place in Panmure Street that taught shorthand and type-writing. Even then I think I knew that this was not really the kind of job for me, but it was a job and if I didn't like it, after I was trained up, I could look for some other office work.

In those days your parents could legitimately say to you: 'Yehr no hingin aboot here daen nothin, yeh'll get yehrsel a joab.' Because you *could* look around and get a job, and there *were* jobs to go and look for. Then if you didn't like it, you *could* seek elsewhere.

There were five-year apprenticeships for young boys and by the end of that time they had become really good experienced tradesmen. Also, I was fortunate indeed that my parents were in the position that I could get a job that was lower paid, and take the time to get trained.

I was also lucky that they encouraged me (indeed all of us) to be the best we could and that if we wanted something, then we should work hard and get it. My father used to say: 'If yehr no rich that's nae crime. But then the wey tae get whit yeh really want is education. Go oot an decide whit yeh want. Then find the wey tae dae it.'

And that had been his philosophy all along with us. If I'd said I wanted to be an astronaut, he'd have got in touch with NASA. But he was the age he was then, and knew what he knew. And I was the age I was then, and didn't know what I was certain I did know.

So with that well-thought-out logic in mind, I decided I wanted to be a 'real' worker.

After discussions with my pal (who also worked in an office) we decided that we did indeed want to give the mills a try. In those days, office workers were not paid well at all. So we'd go and train to be weavers and make ourselves some good money.

This is the bit where if I'd been back in the cinema club, that wee yellow bird that the cat was always after, would stick his head round the side of the screen, roll his gi-normous eyes to and fro and twitter OH . . . OH! OH . . . OH! OH . . . OH! And you just knew that cat would ignore him entirely and just carry on!

So, when I made the 'real worker' announcement it went down (surprise, surprise) like a lead balloon with my father, and he took some persuading. But my mother took a more philosophical stance.

My mother had worked in the mills in Dundee most of her life until she got married and had us. Then she brought us up and went back part-time for the extra money when we were all older. She was a jute reeler/winder and that was very hard work.

One of my lasting memories of her was when I would go down to meet her to have lunch in the mill canteen, and I would stand at the lodge door and watch until she appeared at the open door of the mill.

She would go over to the wall to get her coat from one of the hangers, but before she put her coat on she would 'switch herself down'. They had brushes made up of twine, I think it was, and they used to switch their hair, shoulders, and clothes . . . to get rid of the stoor (dust) that had gathered. Once when she hadn't switched it off, I have even seen a thin line of this dust lying along the tops of my mother's eyelashes.

All that done, she'd appear with a wave and a smile (as ever) and off we'd go.

So when I announced that I wanted to go and make real money, and that I didn't like that office in any case, she just said: 'Well, they say some o' the best lessons in life are the ains yeh learn yehrsel, so aff yeh pop. It could be the makin's o' yeh.' So off I popped to be made, thus beginning my sojourn in the mills in Dundee, just like some of the women (and men) in my family before me. And, of course, like countless other Dundonians back then.

I was more fortunate in that by the time I had started there were Health and Safety regulations: no weekend working that was not overtime, and a five-day week, 7.30 a.m. until 5 p.m., if I remember, with two tea breaks of ten minutes, and about thirty minutes for your lunch.

A far cry from my Auntie Mary and my grandmother's time.

So my mother duly wakened me up early that first morning for the 'workers' bus' and off I went, piecey-time roll in hand, my own cup, and a determination to 'mak a lot o' money'.

The mill I worked in was set on a brae and was a flax mill, which wasn't nearly as 'stoorie' as the jute mills, but there was still a certain amount of dust in the air. At least it wasn't as visible.

In the weeks to come, I was to run like a mad thing up that works' brae to get in before the bummer calling you to work stopped, because that meant you were late and you got money docked from your wages.

The later you were, the more money you lost. And even after you lost money, you still got into trouble if the gaffer caught you coming in late too often.

My first and everlasting impression of that mill was the *noise*. It was quite literally deafening, like the roar of a train engine, or an aeroplane, that just never moved off.

By the time I started, they had begun issuing earplugs, which the young in their infinite wisdom wore, or didn't wear, and the older workers in the main just ignored. My own mother was very hard of hearing, and I am sure her hearing loss was due to industrial deafness.

I learned to 'speak with my hands' because the only other way you could be heard was to cup your hands over the side of the person's face and shout into their ear. Therefore, if they were any distance away, you'd have *that* as a means of communication. But mill workers had their own language and could speak to each other as long as they could see each other.

Tea breaks were taken sitting down on a stool (if you had one, the wooden work passage if you didn't). The bummer went and you stopped, then the bummer went and you started back to work.

I was trained for six weeks then 'put on' with an experienced weaver to assist her. The quicker I learned, the sooner I got my own set of looms. And that happened in due course.

To this day I think piece workers and bonus workers should get a medal, never mind the extra money!

It was a case of work and more work, and that was how you earned the good money, through bonus payments, because, as a matter of fact, the basic wage for these workers was low, and it was the bonus that brought the wages up, and for that you worked very hard indeed.

So now I had 'meh ain set o' looms', eight in total, and I did indeed 'run up an doon the pass a' day lang', keeping those machines fed. And now I was a real worker, making money, was I ecstatic?

I think not. I had never worked so hard in my life.

So then . . . on to plan B. How to set about creating a get-out-of-jail-clause. I knew better than to even say at home that I didn't like the job. I had been warned from He-who-means-it: 'If yeh dinna like this work, then dinna come in here greetin tae yehr mither, after leavin a perfectly guid joab. An certainly *don't* leave it until yeh've got yerhsel another joab.' So that's exactly what I did.

Once again I followed a well-trodden Dundonian route to work for a certain watch company; I went back to office work and back into training for a job that was to last me for years to come.

I had worked in the mills for just over a year, and although I didn't like the work that much, I liked most of the folk I met and worked with there: the tenters who looked after the looms; the oil man who took care of your looms by making sure the wheels and cogs were well oiled; the older weavers who were 'spare hands' and went round helping everybody. The mill was a hive of industry, its own wee world.

The only person who was not all that popular was the lodge keeper, because he'd to mark you in, out, or late. But then again here we are back at chief cinema club ushers, Parkies and Watchies. I guess someone had to do those jobs, right enough!

I loved the laughs I had when I was a weaver, and there were plenty. I loved being with the people there and hearing the 'crack', and the arguments about who had gotten the best yarn to work with, or not, as was the case. And, of course, the comradeship it provided.

They were a strong, hard-working breed of folk (it was a female dominated environment) who in the main just got on with it. They certainly never got paid enough, but they worked for every penny they did get. Even as I write this all these years on, I have nothing but respect and admiration for them all.

And at last, I understood my father's fondness for 'The Yaird'.

So I moved on. I was trained for a job that was to be my working world for many a year to come, although I never knew that at the time.

What I was sure of by then was that I wouldn't ever like a job that I had to sit down at a desk all day long ('Ach away yeh go,' I hear my mother say), but I found my niche eventually in computing and remained in that industry for most of my working life.

I tell folk I went into computing as a punch-card operator when the machines didn't plug into the wall. When I retired they were plugging into your ear hole and the whole world.

As I speak about the start of my own working life I am reminded how utterly worlds apart it was from that of my parents, my grandparents and my Great-Auntie Mary, and all the rest.

My Grandmother and my Auntie Mary worked in the mills from their early years as part-timers, and for all their working lives. My mother was in the jute mills when she wasn't much older than thirteen.

My father was more fortunate than some back then, in that he had one of the newer trades as an electrician, but he still worked much of his life outside, going in and out of the bowels of the ships, especially in the winter cold of the docks in Dundee. He was the one who instilled in us a pride in ourselves, and a belief that we could do anything we set our minds to. And we all knew that they'd both move Heaven and Earth to help us get there.

I feel, however, I have to leave the last word to my mother, who made me laugh and was on my side no matter what!

My mother always looked for the good in everybody, and could find the funny side in almost anything. And I hear her yet:

'Mae, this is no a rehearsal. Yeh kin get on weh livin, or yeh kin get on weh deein. In the end it's aye doon tae yehrsel.'

Amen tae that, Mother!

# THE PEHRTY'S OWER –
# EH'M AFF HAME

Well here we are, at the end of this particular part of my Memory Lane, signposted *'Dundee – Age five to seventeen'*. If you've stuck with me this far, thanks very much. I sincerely hope you've enjoyed yourself.

What struck me, as my faithful keyboard and I journeyed our way through telling these stories, was just how quickly I slipped back into yester-year, and how quickly my family slipped through me, via my keyboard, and settled into their new role as a book. I've had the joy of feeling somehow closer to them in a completely new way.

I've always believed that all the generations that came before are still a huge part of us; we can't see or touch them anymore, but that doesn't mean they're gone and forgotten. So I hope they enjoyed themselves as well.

You know, it's also made me think about how ordinary working folk in Dundee have come a long way from when I was five years of age (which was sixty-four years ago actually).

Writing these memories (memoirs if you're famous) brought home to me just *how* far we've travelled from then until now.

I was around before ordinary working-class homes had

televisions, telephones, refrigerators, microwaves or washing machines. I think I only knew a couple of folk who had a car. To us, back in the 1940s, these modern everyday items were classed as 'luxury goods'.

Lots of houses in Dundee didn't have electricity. Most street lighting was gas, and being a lamp lighter (a 'leerie') was a proper job. Sometimes the leerie would knock on folks' windows and waken them up for their work as well, or that could be separate employment for someone (a 'chapper-upper').

Take a simple thing like boiling a kettle. When I was a kid that meant: using a kettle for every drop of hot water we needed; keeping the shilling/penny meter stocked so that you could light the gas to boil the kettle; and having matches to light the gas ring. And all that just for a cup of tea.

Now you can just switch on the kettle (which even has water levels to tell you how many cups you'll get from that particular amount of water, which I duly ignore), and hey presto, you're done and dusted. You want a wash, jump in the bath or shower. You want to clean the carpets, there's no throwing your carpets over the rope in the greenie and batter-ing away with a carpet beater, just switch on the Hoover and off you go! Mind you, there were no fitted carpets back then either. You would have had right sore back trying to fling them over a rope in the back greenie.

No prizes for guessing which I think is best!

I had at least ten jobs before I settled down with Dundee Corporation (Tayside Region now) in their new computer section as a punch card operator.

The week I started with Dundee Corporation (The 'Corpie'), someone was retiring after thirty years or so, and I remember sitting at that 'cheerio cup of tea do' thinking: 'Wid yeh no put a bullet up yehr nose if yeh wir in the same place fir thirty years?' Approximately thirty years later, I was retiring, and I bet there was someone thinking exactly the same thing. But who can guarantee thirty years in any job now?

But, and here's what's never changed, no matter how clever technology has become, in Dundee or anywhere else, nothing is ever accomplished without help and communication from other human beings. No matter how sophisticated the world gets, it can't replace us. Well, not with anything half as good!

And here's something else I just thought about: cashline machines. They're dotted all over Dundee now as we've monetarily moved forward (and I use the word 'forward' reservedly here) to electronic funds. My father never even had an electric shaver at one time, never mind electronic money, that in his opinion, 'jist kids yeh on that yehr better aff than yeh are.' Although I must admit it's all very convenient.

But some of the biggest changes have been in Dundee itself.

Gone is the Royal Arch that sat beside the Empress Ballroom; gone is the Overgate, the Wellgate and the Wellgate steps; M'Gills at the top of the steps; and that's only to name a few.

Oh! And the Green's Playhouse Cinema (it's a bingo hall now, so it's still providing entertainment for Dundonians), used to have a very posh entrance with marble stairs and floors, and a restaurant just inside the entrance where you could have a tea or a coffee.

My father was one of the electricians who worked on the Green's Playhouse when they were installing the electrics, and everybody thought it was extremely posh!

Now, instead of loads of wee cinemas we have the multiplexes. But I still love 'the pictures'. Some of the modern computerised graphics are splendid indeed. I thought I'd died and gone to cinema-club heaven when I saw the first Harry Potter film.

I think Dundee has regenerated very well over my lifetime. We have a new Wellgate; a new Overgate; Verdant Works (one of the oldest jute mills in Scotland) has been turned into a Museum; Discovery Quay with its museum and Captain Scott's boat; the DCA arts and cinema complex; bigger shopping centres than any of us could have imagined; and that's to name but a few of the major changes. Oh yes, and buses that have kneeling steps so that you can get the Tansad on (Oops! Buggie).

And what about our newly renovated Museum in Albert Square? That building looks absolutely magnificent. I'm dying to get a nosey inside. Before the outside looked like it needed a 'guid wash an brush up'. Now, it looks like it's got on a posh wedding outfit.

When the museum re-opens, they'll have to shoot the pigeons that try to land (or whatever) on the splendid Burns Statue that sits just outside the grand entrance, as it *'wid niver do, tae hiv a doo, daein a doo-doo on Rabbies heid'*.

We're to have a brand spanking new Council Swimming Complex in the not-too-distant future. A far cry from the swimming baths I used to go to with my father in the 1940s. You used to have to queue up to get in back then. I have always loved swimming and look forward to the new complex opening.

Then there are the new Waterfront Development plans. I think I'll be ancient when they're completed, but hopefully they'll have invented zimmers that float (or whish) along, so that I don't have to walk all the way along the waterfront. That might be a new Monkeys' Parade for 2030!

There have been many changes in Dundee since the days of my childhood and when I look in the mirror there's been just as many changes in me. I'm very proud to be a Dundonian!

And you know what I love about Dundee the most? The

feeling that I'm where I'm *meant* to be. When I'm on holiday, especially when I've been abroad, I love coming back to Dundee and getting into a taxi where the taxi driver gabs away to you, asks how the holiday went, and so on. Think how many places in the world that never happens.

And no matter where I am, I always *want* to come home. And no matter how long I live, that's what Dundee will always mean to me – Home! Think of how many people all over the world can't say that!

As far as I'm concerned, I'm only just round the corner from the signpost in Memory Lane that says *'Dundee – Age five to seventeen'*, and who knows what other adventures are out there just waiting for the both of us?

Someone, somewhere, once wrote: *'There are no endings, only more beginnings.'*

Or, as my mother would've said: 'Right that's that done weh! Whit are weh waitin fir? Wagons Ho!'